A God for All Seasons

Inspiration and Reflection for All Times

Cover design by Bradley Wind
Author photo by Jennifer King

Printed in the United States of America.

Booklocker.com, Inc.
2012

A God for All Seasons

Inspiration and Reflection for All Times

Patti Tingen

Anita,
Blessings in
every season!
Patti
2019

Dedication

Blessed God—for your faithfulness in every season of my life

Knick fans everywhere—for your encouragement to me to keep writing

My authonomy friends—for your invaluable suggestions and support

Doug—for sharing the journey with me

Table of Contents

Introduction .... **ix**

WINTER **1**

December: A time to hope 3
January: A time to renew 11
February: A time to wait 19

SPRING **27**

March: A time to change 29
April: A time to plant 37
May: A time to trust 43

SUMMER **51**

June: A time to give 53
July: A time to celebrate 59
August: A time to rest 67

AUTUMN **75**

September: A time to harvest 77
October: A time to believe 83
November: A time to thank 91

Epilogue: A time to reflect **97**

Introduction

"There is a time for everything,
a season for every activity under heaven.
A time to be born and a time to die.
A time to plant and a time to harvest.
A time to kill and a time to heal.
A time to tear down and a time to rebuild.
A time to cry and a time to laugh.
A time to grieve and a time to dance.
A time to scatter stones and a time to gather stones.
A time to embrace and a time to turn away.
A time to search and a time to lose.
A time to keep and a time to throw away.
A time to tear and a time to mend.
A time to be quiet and a time to speak up.
A time to love and a time to hate.
A time for war and a time for peace."

Ecclesiastes 3:1-8 (NLT)

Life is never static. Physical, emotional, financial and spiritual ups and downs are all a part of this journey called life. More than ever before, I'm seeing how God is with us for the entire journey, through all of the highs and lows.

The seasons of the year have often been used as pictures of life; I think the months are also such pictures. Walk with me through the seasons and their months, no matter where you need to start—by the calendar or by your life-season.

Much of my adulthood has been peppered with a variety of struggles and times spent in the cold winter season. As I am now emerging into the warmth and light of spring, I'm realizing that I have learned well how to exist in the darkness. My desire is also to flourish in the blooming seasons.

Please join me in this year of exploration and reflection. May you find hope and encouragement in every month—and in every season.

It's time.

WINTER

*"As long as the earth remains, there will be planting and harvest, cold and heat, summer and **winter**, day and night."* Genesis 8:22 (NLT)

Snowflakes gently falling, icicles glistening, wood fires crackling... some of the sights and sounds of winter. Holiday celebrations and children cavorting in the snow can bring much laughter and joy to our souls. Some of my wintertime favorites include comfy sweaters, fuzzy blankets and a steaming cup of cocoa. And of course, a purring kitty to snuggle in my lap. All these help to warm my heart and lift my spirits.

In many ways, winter is a beautiful season. It can also be a very difficult time to endure. The harsh winds, long dark nights and icy temperatures can leave us longing for the light and warmth of spring. Handling the physical aspects of winter is trying enough—but when we also "winter" spiritually, the darkness can become almost unbearable. This can be especially difficult if our "winter" continues on long past the season's end date on the calendar.

Whether we like it or not, we will continue to have winters— in one way or another. But there is much we can learn in winter that can't be acquired in any other season. So in spite of the cold, in spite of the darkness, there is reason to not give up. For winter can bring us hope—it is a chance to renew—and it can be an occasion to wait.

These are the times of winter.

December: A time to hope

*"Always be prepared to give an answer to everyone who asks you to give the reason for the **hope** that you have."* 1 Peter 3:15 (NIV)

December—the season of joy. Perhaps for some. For others, it is a time of deep sadness, sorrow and hopelessness. According to the National Mental Health Association, more than one million Americans suffer from depression during December and more people attempt suicide in this month than at any other time of the year.

December surely can bring suffocating darkness. It can also bring an opportunity for hope. When the dark shadows close in around us, when all seems meaningless, when we feel like we cannot go on for one more moment—Jesus is our hope.

The Gospel of John tells us that Jesus is the light that the darkness could not overcome. "The Word gave life to everything that was created, and His life brought light to everyone. The light shines in the darkness, and the darkness can never extinguish it." John 1:4-5 (NLT)

Therefore, if Jesus lives in us—the darkness cannot overcome us either. It is in His name that we can trust, in His name that we can believe, and by His grace alone that we can find the courage to go on.

Moving from darkness to light can be a difficult process. But only when we have endured the blackest of nights and the darkest of days can we truly appreciate the light. For without the contrast, the brightness and warmth of better days are taken for granted and sorely underappreciated.

Only in the coldest, most desolate, difficult "Decembers" of my life did I actually learn what it means to hope. Not an "I hope they have ice cream at the party tonight" hope. This was an end-of-my-rope, sliver-of-light, hanging-on-by-a-thread, clinging, desperate, longing hope. A hope that can only be found in winter.

Over the course of a five-year period, my husband Doug and I walked through some of our darkest days together. A promising dream and eventual disappointment of not succeeding in starting a business, dire financial straits, the selling of our home, the loss of our beloved cat Knickerbocker, the passing of my Grandmother, the death of Doug's twin brother, unemployment, physical illness, emotional struggles and more disappointment than I could fathom were some of what greeted us during those long, bleak years.

After our situation had improved somewhat, I completed one of those stress scales where you answer yes or no to a list of stress-producing events resulting in a total score. (Like you actually need a test to tell you whether or not you're stressed.) Still, I was curious as to what the experts would say my stress level was during that time. With a rating of 300 and above indicating very high stress, I scored 481 points!

I can honestly say that those years were both the hardest and yet the most precious that I have ever experienced. For nothing can compare to the gut-wrenching process of drawing near, pressing in, and clutching onto God when little else is left. Those are the times when one flicker of flame, one spark of light, one glimmer of hope can bring enough courage to continue on. Sometimes those flickers and sparks are seen or felt in an emotional way; other times they are made more tangible.

Worry threatened regularly as Doug set out to start his own business. It was definitely a faith adventure as we were stretched financially, emotionally and spiritually. Listening to a new CD I had just purchased bolstered my hopes. At the end of the song by Ray Boltz titled "I Think I See Gold," I heard a crackling sound, which I likened to confirmation that we were indeed in the fire. By God's grace, I felt it was yet one more assurance that though this process was more difficult than we had ever imagined, we were being transformed and refined and would come out in the end shining pure as gold.

Excited for Doug to also hear the song, I removed the CD from the computer where I had just listened to it through headphones and headed to the living room to play it for him on our stereo. He also enjoyed the song and remarked that he especially liked the crackling sound at the end. "It sounds like a fire," he said.

"I know; isn't that awesome?"

Well, I listened to that song countless times as our wearisome journey continued—but no matter what device I used, never again did I hear the cracks and pops of that spiritual fire. But our refining process continued, growing more difficult with each passing day.

Some months later, fears were rising again as our financial situation worsened and the promise of success looked more doubtful than ever. Wondering yet again if it was time to close the book on this dream, I felt drawn to look out the window at the back of our house. Our row of in-ground lights was continually shorting out, so I gave up long ago on even replacing the bulbs. In fact, I wasn't even sure if there were still any bulbs in the lamps. Nevertheless, on this one remarkable night, hope arose from deep within, as I gazed at the lights shining brightly on our little patio. And I was reassured once again, that no matter how difficult our journeys may be—the light of God's promises, whether by fire or lamp, can always be trusted.

Sometimes our Lord shines through boldly and beautifully; other times He seems to be nowhere in sight. A few years after we had sold our home and moved to a rental unit, new neighbors moved into the property adjoining ours. They seemed to be quite nice. They also smoked cigarettes—continuously. Their friends smoked, their two sons smoked, their sons' friends smoked, everyone who entered that house seemed to smoke. In fact, when absolutely no one was home, the place smoked all by itself!

We knew all of this because the smoke would immediately make its way over to our place. It came through the heating and air conditioning vents, it came into the basement, it seeped right through the walls. At all hours of the day and night. One Saturday afternoon, Doug could not cope with it for one more minute. Opening the door to my husband's impassioned petitions to please give us a break, our confused neighbor stammered, "But we were sleeping!"

On the day these folks moved in, there was a literal cloud in our front room. Grabbing my car keys and a large box of tissues, I headed out the back door. I told Doug not to worry, that I would be okay and I would come back, but that right then, I needed to go away. Driving aimlessly for a few minutes, I headed out of town and shortly pulled into the parking lot of a small church.

I tried yelling at God for a bit but that proved rather ineffective. By then my bawling had pretty much ceased and the tears wouldn't even come anymore. Yet the hurt and frustration permeated every fiber of my being. "Haven't I been through enough already? And now this?!"

I was hopefully anticipating some sort of miraculous encounter. Where a stranger, perchance even an angel, would suddenly appear, note my obvious distress and bring me prophetic, soothing words of encouragement, comfort and hope. I waited—and I waited—and I paced outside the car a little—and I tried to muster up some more tears. But there was no stranger; there was no angel. Only two middle-aged women across the parking lot who barely gave me a passing glance. Then from deep inside, a small voice I recognized calmly said, "Are you done now?"

The "smoking people," as we came to call them, eventually moved. And all the smoke moved with them. There was not one trace left behind. Just as miraculous, the smoke didn't stick when they *did* live next door. Even when the young folks had their "Friday night smoke fests" and a haze hung in our living room like a 1970's bowling alley, the odor did not cling to our possessions or to us. Though our eyes and throats burned from the acrid odor, if we left the immediate vicinity, nothing on our person smelled—not our clothing, not our hair, not one thing. Moreover, when the party ended and the smoke eventually cleared, there was not a trace left behind. Not in the carpet, not on our furniture, not even on our coats that hung in a wardrobe where the heaviest smoke came through.

Hmmmm… reminds me of another story where the smoke didn't stick. "So Shadrach, Meshach, and Abednego stepped out of the fire. Then the high officers, officials, governors, and advisers crowded around them and saw that the fire had not touched them. Not a hair on their heads was singed, and their clothing was not scorched. They didn't even smell of smoke!" Daniel 3:26-27 (NLT)

God cares for us even when it feels like He is a million miles away. He knows our struggles and He is with us. His protection covers us head to toe. "When you go through deep waters, I will be with you. When you go through rivers of difficulty, you will not drown. When you walk through the fire of oppression, you will not be burned up; the flames will not consume you." Isaiah 43:2 (NLT)

Notice that this scripture says, "*When* you go through," not *if* you go through. We WILL go through difficulties; it's a part of the fallen world that we live in. I don't suggest you go looking for trouble, but don't rail against it when it comes. Let out the anger and frustration as you need to, but then press back into God. Run to Jesus, not away from Him. Because honestly—where else is there to go? Plenty of places actually, but where else is there that will truly help in the end? Don't waste precious time and energy trying to escape. You might find some temporary pleasure but eventually, the emptiness inside you will be darker and even more hopeless than before.

Facing "winter" can be the most difficult season of all. So many people leave the church and run away from their faith when they hit that wall. Please don't run away. Sometimes the fire burns a long, long time before the smoke clears, but do not give up. Find your sliver of light and cling to it with every fiber of your being. Claim one verse of scripture that speaks to you and repeat it to yourself endlessly. Say it silently or shout it from the rooftops. Remind yourself over and over again that the promise is true and that you are going to believe it no matter what—for however long it takes.

Sometimes December lasts much longer than 31 days. But also notice that the scripture from Isaiah talks about going through. It might take a very long time, but there is another side and if we persevere, eventually we will emerge from the river or the flames. While we are there, we can trust—and we can hope.

Horatio G. Spafford, who penned the famous hymn "It Is Well with My Soul," knew how to hope in the midst of difficulty. According to Robert J. Morgan in his book, "Then Sings My Soul," Horatio lost a fortune in real estate during the great Chicago fire. About that same time, his only son died of scarlet fever. Two years later, his four daughters perished in a shipwreck and his wife barely survived. Still he wrote, "It is well with my soul."

Certainly, Horatio could not have felt well emotionally or physically; nothing in his life at that time was well. So how could he possibly compose those words? Because in the very core of his being, in the depths of his soul—there was hope. It might have been only a flicker, or the tiniest flame, but some measure of hope burned deep inside his soul—and in his soul—it was well.

In the soul is where our hope resides. That is where the power to persevere lives. It is not in our minds, not in our emotions, and not in our physical abilities. It is in our souls. So learn to nurture your soul. Spend time seeking God and praising Him no matter the season in which you find yourself. Find a church where you can learn and develop your faith. Fellowship with other believers; serve and care for other people.

All of these activities will help to develop your faith and encourage your soul. And you will be better prepared and equipped when the harsh winds of winter begin to blow. Then when December's cold, dark nights descend, when all seems lost, when nothing makes sense, it will be well. Because in your soul, you'll find hope. And as long as you have hope—endurance, perseverance and faith will follow. So find your hope this December—then prepare for a time of renewal.

January: A time to renew

*"That is why we never give up. Though our bodies are dying, our spirits are being **renewed** every day."* 2 Corinthians 4:16 (NLT)

It's January—a brand new year! You might still be carrying concerns and burdens from previous times, but there's just something stirring and hopeful about the beginning of another year. In Christ, it is never too late to start over. Each new year truly is an opportunity to begin anew. In fact, every moment holds an invitation to renew our minds, bodies and spirits.

If you have ever been to a gym, you know that January is when all the new people show up. Anxious to keep their resolutions to finally lose some weight, out-of-shape folks come out en masse to take on the challenge of changing their bodies. Then all too quickly, most of these new converts give up as their aching limbs and sore muscles cry out for relief.

Remaking ourselves physically is extremely difficult. It takes time, perseverance, and a steadfast desire for change. Spiritual transformation, renewing our spirits and souls, is also quite challenging. Yet it holds far greater rewards.

"Spend your time and energy in training yourself for spiritual fitness. Physical exercise has some value, but spiritual exercise is much more important, for it promises a reward in both this life and the next." 1 Timothy 4:7b-8 (NLT)

As we begin this new year, why not consider giving ourselves an extreme *spiritual* makeover? Our spirits can be made new no matter what our age or physical condition. And a spiritual makeover

11

will result in truer and more lasting beauty than any physical transformation could ever accomplish. So let's get started...

Many physical makeovers include plastic surgery on one's nose—usually to make it smaller. But why would a spiritual nose job be of benefit and how might that look?

Most, if not all of us, have probably had occasions where we have had our noses in the air. Perhaps not literally, but in our minds or our hearts, we may have thought we were better than someone else was. I know I can often judge others and place myself above those around me. Then there are the brown-nosers—always trying to work their way to the top by stepping on those beneath them.

If you have struggled in this area, then a spiritual makeover on your nose might be helpful. Philippians gives us a glimpse of the post-surgical outcome. "Don't be selfish; don't live to make a good impression on others. Be humble, thinking of others as better than yourself. Don't think only about your own affairs, but be interested in others, too, and what they are doing." Philippians 2:3-4 (NLT)

Often accompanying a nose job is the desire for a face-lift. In this operation, the surgeon pulls everything up, smoothing out the skin, and all the sags, wrinkles and lines seem to magically vanish. In Proverbs, we see the key to a spiritual facelift. "A joyful heart makes a cheerful face, but when the heart is sad, the spirit is broken." Proverbs 15:13 (NAS)

Our faces reveal the state of our hearts. And it has absolutely nothing to do with how healthy we are, how much money we have, or the problems with which we may or may not be dealing. Certainly, it's easier to smile when things are going well. But if we are truly trusting God, our hearts will be joyful and it will show on our faces.

I vividly recall seeing a woman in the middle of a losing battle with 4th stage cancer who just seemed to be glowing. The joy in her heart lifted her face—and there was no plastic surgery necessary.

Another area needing extreme transformation is our mouths. Cosmetic dentistry can leave one with a perfect, brilliantly white smile. However, what is truly important is what passes through those teeth and lips. If we allow God to renew our mouths, we will follow these instructions from Ephesians. "Do not let any unwholesome talk come out of your mouths, but only what is helpful for building others up according to their needs, that it may benefit those who listen." Ephesians 4:29 (NIV)

Proverbs gives us some good advice as well. "Words satisfy the soul as food satisfies the stomach; the right words on a person's lips bring satisfaction. Those who love to talk will experience the consequences, for the tongue can kill or nourish life." Proverbs 18:20-21 (NLT)

There are numerous scriptures about how to use our tongues in ways that will glorify God and bless others. Probably more than any other part of our bodies, how we use our mouths may have the most significant impact on those around us. Maybe as we brush our teeth each morning, we can ask God to make over our mouths, that we would use them to honor Him that day.

The next step in our spiritual renewal is with our eyes. Laser surgery can result in never needing to wear thick, unattractive glasses again. Yet while we may be able to view the world perfectly clearly without spectacles, without a spiritual makeover—the only world we will be able to see is in the natural. Let's look at how we can view the world and our circumstances through the vision that can only come from having a relationship with Christ.

Continuing with our title verse from 2 Corinthians, the Bible says: "For our present troubles are quite small and won't last very long. Yet they produce for us an immeasurably great glory that will last forever! So we don't look at the troubles we can see right now; rather, we look forward to what we have not yet seen. For the troubles we see will soon be over, but the joys to come will last forever." 2 Corinthians 4:17-18 (NLT)

With God's vision, we can look past all of the pain, heartache and trouble that comes with life. For we can see into eternity, where we will live in never-ending glory! When we draw on that hope and the strength that comes from Jesus, we can make it through each day no matter what might be happening in our physical lives.

After a makeover, most people don't want to wear their same old, tired, ill-fitting clothes hanging in their closets. They desire a new wardrobe. So they may run off to a swanky boutique in order to find some outfits that would best show off their new looks. But what does it look like to have a spiritual makeover completed on our wardrobes? Scripture tells us in Colossians.

"Since God chose you to be the holy people whom he loves, you must clothe yourselves with tenderhearted mercy, kindness, humility, gentleness, and patience. You must make allowance for each other's faults and forgive the person who offends you. Remember, the Lord forgave you, so you must forgive others. And the most important piece of clothing you must wear is love. Love is what binds us all together in perfect harmony." Colossians 3:12-14 (NLT)

What we wear on the inside is of far greater value than an expensive physical wardrobe. Yet how much time, effort and money often goes into making sure we're wearing the latest styles in order to look appealing to others and create a favorable impression?

God, the greatest fashion designer of all, places far greater emphasis on our spiritual clothing. Mercy, kindness, humility, gentleness and patience. If we wore those every day, can you imagine the compliments we would receive? That is the kind of clothing I want to wear, but far too often, I do not. I imagine most of us struggle in this area. We need to make a conscious effort, taking as much and probably more care each day in getting dressed spiritually than we do physically.

So in the same way that we can remember to make over our mouths when we brush our teeth, we can also consider our spiritual clothing when we get dressed in the morning. Ephesians also talks about this and likens it to putting on our spiritual armor.

"Use every piece of God's armor to resist the enemy in the time of evil, so that after the battle you will still be standing firm. Stand your ground, putting on the sturdy belt of truth and the body armor of God's righteousness. For shoes, put on the peace that comes from the Good News, so that you will be fully prepared. In every battle you will need faith as your shield to stop the fiery arrows aimed at you by Satan. Put on your salvation as your helmet, and take the sword of the Spirit, which is the Word of God. Pray at all times and on every occasion in the power of the Holy Spirit. Stay alert and be persistent in your prayers for all Christians everywhere." Ephesians 6:13-18 (NLT)

Christ has already won the battle, however our spiritual clothing remains essential. If we choose daily to clothe ourselves with these wardrobes—we will look fabulous—without ever spending a penny.

In this month of renewal, let's continue with our makeover theme by exploring the differences between a physical and a spiritual transformation. First, a physical makeover is man-made. A surgeon, dentist or hair stylist is using his or her God-given gifts, but *they* are the source of change to all those who receive their services.

A spiritual makeover is God-made. Whether it is salvation for a new believer or the ongoing work of transformation that happens as we walk in relationship with our Lord, God accomplishes the changes to our lives. No man or woman, in and of himself or herself, can do that for us.

Also, consider that a physical makeover is temporary, but a spiritual makeover lasts forever. The novel haircut is going to grow out, the stylish clothing will become worn, and even with plastic surgery, there are areas that will eventually start wrinkling and sagging again. It is just a matter of time.

But the changes we allow God to make in our spiritual lives continue for all eternity. They're timeless. This is why it is so important to allow God to renew us. Because if we don't, we will live forever with the results of the choices we have made.

Another difference between these transformations is that a physical makeover changes us from the outside-in, but a spiritual makeover alters us from the inside-out. People who have received a physical makeover may remark how differently they feel inside as a result of the dramatic changes in their outward appearances. However, their transformations began with the outside changes.

In our spiritual lives, God is continually changing us inside. He is shaping and renewing our hearts, minds, and thoughts—all of the inside workings. As these inward changes are made, our lives then begin to change on the outside. In how we speak, the things we do, and in the ways we treat others. The outward manifestations in how we conduct ourselves are a result of the internal changes.

Lastly, a physical makeover is expensive while a spiritual makeover is a gift. Consider how much money is spent, surgery or not, on trying to make ourselves look better physically. While there is absolutely nothing wrong with trying to look our best, the Bible says we judge each other by outward appearances, but the Lord looks at the heart.

The followers of Jesus weren't attracted to Him because of His physical appearance; they followed Him because of who He was inside and because of the love that spilled out from Him to everyone He met. And that love is still spilling out to you and me today.

God cares about our inward changes, and while a spiritual makeover does cost us, it's not in dollars. No matter your social status, the amount of money in your bank account, or how large a house you live in, you are eligible for an extreme spiritual makeover. Our Lord has already chosen each one of us to be made-over in His image. We just need to accept His invitation.

At the start of this new year, what better time to allow God to give you a spiritual makeover? As you go out in joy, peace and humility, your new looks will be noticed and appreciated by family, friends and strangers alike. So let God renew you this January. Then it is time to watch and wait as he continues His transformation the whole year through.

February: A time to wait

*"I **waited** patiently for the Lord to help me, and He turned to me and heard my cry. He lifted me out of the pit of despair, out of the mud and the mire. He set my feet on solid ground and steadied me as I walked along. He has given me a new song to sing, a hymn of praise to our God. Many will see what He has done and be astounded. They will put their trust in the Lord."* Psalm 40:1-3 (NLT)

Hopefully you've taken some positive steps with the beginnings of a new year. If so, you are probably expecting to see the results of your renewal. And well you should. Yet often the outcomes do not come nearly as quickly as we might hope. In our world of instant gratification, we expect rapid results, speedy solutions and immediate answers. But what if the changes don't occur instantaneously?

Just as winter drags on, the journey of faith can continue to be difficult, especially if we are in a place of anticipation. Though February is the shortest of months, those 28 or 29 days can feel endless and the hope of spring can seem dim indeed. With the ground still frozen, bare branches covered in ice, there is little to do but wait.

And waiting is anything but easy. Perhaps one reason it is so challenging is that it seems like a waste of time. When we wait, we feel as though we're not being productive, we're not accomplishing anything and we're not making any progress. It appears as if we are doing nothing—we're simply....waiting.

However, we need to recognize that "wait" is a verb. And verbs are action words. So when we wait, we are doing something.

We're waiting. It's an activity. It might not be as fun or exciting as some other pursuits, but it is an activity nonetheless.

Upon realizing this, I began to look at waiting with new eyes. I started to understand that it could be an active and productive time given the right perspective. This is very important because God loves waiting—and perhaps He wants us to learn to love it too.

The Bible is full of famous waiters. The scriptures tell us story after story of everyday people who God used in extraordinary ways. Yet very often, they waited an exceedingly long time for that moment to come.

Abraham, for example, was already seventy-five years old when God first called him. Twenty-five years later, his wife Sarah, at ninety years of age, gave birth to their son Isaac. It was a promise fulfilled but it was a very, very long time in coming. I imagine for Abraham and Sarah, those were years of wondering, of hoping, of believing, of doubting. Waiting is not easy—even if you're a famous Bible character.

But can you imagine their delight at the birth of their miracle-baby? What a celebration they must have had! Delirious with joy, I imagine they felt it was worth the wait.

That is one of the "wonders of waiting." It will be worth it in the end. It will all be worth it. All the sorrow, all the heartache, all the tears. Joy will replace them all.

Psalm 30 says, "You have turned my mourning into joyful dancing. You have taken away my clothes of mourning and clothed me with joy, that I might sing praises to You and not be silent. O Lord my God, I will give you thanks forever!" Psalm 30:11-12 (NLT)

During the many dark years that Doug and I endured, numerous influences sustained me. One of them was a promise Doug received from a friend during a time of prayer. She prophesied, "In the darkness, He is near you. In the solitude, He is there. In the heaviness of life, He is with you. In the trials, depression and fear, He holds you. And in the victory, He will celebrate with you."

I typed up those words, printed them out and hung the paper on our refrigerator. And there it remains these many years later. I have read that passage over and over and over again. Knowing that our Lord Himself is going to celebrate with us has helped me to wait. I can picture God smiling just thinking about it!

Know that God will celebrate in your triumphs too. He will rejoice and sing with you as you delight in His goodness in carrying you through your trials—whatever they may be—and for however long they might last. It will be worth it in the end.

In waiting, we will also find new strength. Be encouraged by this familiar scripture passage from Isaiah. "O Israel, how can you say the Lord does not see your troubles? How can you say God refuses to hear your case? Have you never heard or understood? Don't you know that the Lord is the everlasting God, the Creator of all the earth? He never grows faint or weary. No one can measure the depths of His understanding. He gives power to those who are tired and worn out; He offers strength to the weak. Even youths will become exhausted, and young men will give up. But those who wait on the Lord will find new strength. They will fly high on wings like eagles. They will run and not grow weary. They will walk and not faint." Isaiah 40:27-31 (NLT)

In the natural, waiting exhausts us. It tears us down, beats us up and wears us out. If we wait on our own, in our own power, using our own resources and our own energies, we will never make it to the end. However, if we wait on the Lord, who never grows faint or weary, we will find new strength—an inexhaustible supply given daily like manna straight from Heaven.

After years of waiting and trusting, I came to the place where I felt as though I could not continue. However, knowing that God does all things in an orderly and timely way, I started counting. Ironically, it was February at that time. I discovered that if this leg of our journey would end in May, it would have been forty months. I decided that timing seemed perfect and boldly told God so.

"If it was good enough for the Israelites, it's good enough for us. And You know I'll keep trusting You because I have before—even after I thought things were going to be better. But seriously... seriously... this is it. I can hang on for a few more months, but May has to be it. I'm tellin' ya..." And I could sense God's smile.

In the beginning of May, Doug found a job. Forty months. Forty is the number of testing. If you are still waiting, do not give up. The end may be closer than you know. Wait on the Lord—and let Him give you new strength.

While you're waiting, know too that your needs will be met. That is another of the "wonders of waiting." God gives us this promise in Philippians: "And this same God who takes care of me will supply all your needs from His glorious riches, which have been given to us in Christ Jesus." Philippians 4:19 (NLT)

Our Lord has an endless storehouse—an unlimited supply—of whatever we need. At any time, any place, in any way, God can and will meet our needs. We just need to wait for His timing and then recognize His provision as He supplies it.

1 Kings 17 relates an amazing story of provision. Elijah was a prophet and God told him to go to a certain village and see a widow who would feed him. This poor woman was down to a handful of flour and a little cooking oil in the bottom of her jug.

Certainly in a desperate situation, she says, "I was just gathering a few sticks to cook this last meal and then my son and I will die." But Elijah tells her, "Don't be afraid! Go ahead and cook your 'last meal'—but bake me a little loaf of bread first. Afterward there will still be enough food for you and your son." So she did what

Elijah said and sure enough, she and her son and Elijah continued to eat from that supply of flour and oil for many days. The Bible says, "no matter how much they used, there was always enough left in the containers."

Have you ever had containers like that? I know I have. There have definitely been times when my bottle of shampoo or tube of toothpaste has lasted much longer than it would ordinarily. Our checking account is also a testimony to God's incredible resources.

Month after month, I would sit down, compare the stack of bills to the funds available, and think there was no way the money would reach. Yet just as the widow kept baking bread—she didn't look at how little there was; she just took what she needed and kept going—I kept paying bills. I wrote check after check and my banking system on the computer continued to show that there was money available to pay the next bill.

I don't understand how God stretched our finances as He did. I don't need to know nor do I even want to know. I just know He did. And twice a month for those many years I would take my praise walk down to the corner mailbox and drop the stack in—THUNK! There was always enough. God will meet our needs.

The fourth wonder is that God waits with us. Our Lord will never leave us or forsake us. That is a promise from scripture. At times, it can feel as though we have been abandoned depending on how long we have been waiting or the severity of the trials that we are going through. But Psalm 139 says this: "I can never escape from your Spirit! I can never get away from your presence! If I go up to heaven, You are there; if I go down to the place of the dead, You are there. If I ride the wings of the morning, if I dwell by the farthest oceans, even there Your hand will guide me, and Your strength will support me. I could ask the darkness to hide me and the light around me to become night—but even in darkness I cannot hide from You.

To You the night shines as bright as day. Darkness and light are both alike to You." Psalm 139:7-12 (NLT)

Job is perhaps the most recognized waiter—and sufferer—in all of Scripture. In one day, his oxen and donkeys were stolen, his farmhands were killed, his sheep and shepherds were burned up in a fire, his camels were stolen, his servants were killed, his house collapsed and all his children were dead. And that was just his first test!

The Bible does not tell us how long of a wait Job had before God restored everything to him, but it was obviously much longer than Job would have wished.

And while God was waiting with Job, so were his three friends. In the beginning, they painted a beautiful picture of how to comfort and wait with a friend in need. "When they heard of the tragedy he had suffered, they got together and traveled from their homes to comfort and console him. When they saw Job from a distance, they scarcely recognized him. Wailing loudly, they tore their robes and threw dust into the air over their heads to demonstrate their grief. Then they sat on the ground with him for seven days and nights. And no one said a word, for they saw that his suffering was too great for words." Job 2:11-13 (NLT)

If you have a friend in need—sit with him, cry with her, wait with him—and you don't need to say a word. So many of our friends and church family did that for Doug and me through our period of testing. They waited with us over the long haul—showing us nothing but love. Pure, heartfelt, soul-affirming, heart-rending, hope-inspiring, life-sustaining love! We can never thank them enough.

Waiting can be extremely trying. As a result, our hearts often cry out in frustration. "How long is this trial going to last?" "When will God give me the desires of my heart?" "Why won't this situation ever end?" Always full of love and grace, God hears our petitions as we are waiting and waiting and waiting for Him.

However, we need to recognize that we are not the only ones waiting. Consider this verse from 2nd Peter. "And remember, the Lord is waiting so that people have time to be saved." 2 Peter 3:15 (NLT)

While we are waiting for God, our caring Savior is also lovingly, patiently—waiting for us. Jesus Himself is waiting to return so that more people have time to come to a saving relationship with Him. While we're running off like the prodigal son, wasting our money and our lives foolishly—God is waiting. When we commit the same sin over and over and over again—God is waiting. As we are going our own way, following our own agendas—God is waiting.

The Lord waits and waits and waits for us. He waits for us to come to repentance, waits for us to change our sinful habits, waits for us to love Him fully. God waits for us to serve Him and love Him and care for each other in the ways He has instructed us.

We can't have it both ways. We cannot have our prayers answered, wishes fulfilled, and dreams come true in a "microwave-minute" and then expect God to wait into eternity for us to come to Him and love Him as we should. There's waiting on both sides. And of that, we can be very thankful.

If you desire to have a closer relationship with Jesus, you do not need to wait one more day. If there is someone you need to forgive, if you need to repent and turn from an area of sin that keeps tripping you up, don't wait any longer. Maybe you just need to be more patient as you are waiting for God in some area of your life.

Whatever your area of need this February—keep trusting and keep waiting. Then prepare for a time of change.

SPRING

*"Oh, that we might know the Lord! Let us press on to know Him. He will respond to us as surely as the arrival of dawn or the coming of rains in early **spring**."* Hosea 6:3 (NLT)

W arm breezes blowing, the sweet scent of a gentle rain, tender buds pushing through the ground and bursting into life... some of the sights and sounds of spring. It's finally here! As the rays of sunshine filter down, adding light and warmth to the floral display of color unfolding below, our souls are refreshed and renewed.

Soaking in the beauty of that first balmy day of spring is the best day of the year for me. The sights, sounds and smells of this seasonal change carry a promise like none other. New life seems to be everywhere—flowering trees, newborn animals romping and playing, and the fragrance of grass that has wondrously turned the most vibrant shade of green seemingly overnight.

It feels as though all is right with the world when spring arrives. Seeing the hard, frozen ground yield itself to the earliest flowers, reminds us that even in the darkest of winters, when all seems dead, new life is growing in the unseen places.

Spring can also bring the occasional snowstorm—a reminder that winter will not easily release its grasp on the landscape. Strong winds excellent for kite-flying also remind us that change is in the air. For spring is a season of change—it's the time to plant—and it's an opportunity to trust.

These are the times of spring.

March: A time to change

*"So all of us who have had that veil removed can see and reflect the glory of the Lord. And the Lord—who is the Spirit—makes us more and more like him as we are **changed** into His glorious image."*

2 Corinthians 3:18 (NLT)

"In like a lion, out like a lamb," goes the old saying. Ahh... the ever-changing month of March. Just when we think the warmth of spring is going to remain, along comes one last snowstorm just to prove us wrong. Some days it seems nature can't decide which way to go—to stay with winter or move on into the next seasonal phase. Eventually, spring will arrive to stay. But usually not before a time of back and forth, temperate and chilly, ever shifting and changing period of transition.

Sometimes our lives mirror March. We might be in transition for a number of reasons, perhaps of our own making or due to circumstances beyond our control. At times, we may literally be relocating or going through a physical change due to illness or injury. On other occasions, the change may be emotional or spiritual. Some of us enjoy change and others do not. But no matter our personal opinions on the subject, change is an inevitable part of our lives.

Yet isn't it interesting that the Author of life, the Creator of change, says this about Himself? "Whatever is good and perfect comes down to us from God our Father, who created all the lights in the heavens. **He never changes** or casts a shifting shadow." James 1:17 (NLT) The Bible also says, "Jesus Christ is the same yesterday, today and forever." Hebrews 13:8 (NLT)

If God never changes, then why is it so difficult to figure Him out? It often appears as though He is constantly shifting like the wind. Just when we catch a glimpse of insight into God's character and ways, He seems to disappear like a child playing hide-n-seek. And we're left standing with tightened fists full of nothing, grabbing and reaching, capturing little but air.

Do you think the Lord delights in watching us seek in desperation to pin Him down? I don't believe so. God loves us with a never-ending love. He longs for relationship with us and He desires nothing more than for us to know Him in ever and ever greater ways.

He also stubbornly refuses to let us put Him in a box, so to speak. God is not a vending machine, and He will not for one moment allow us to treat Him like one. We cannot transform Him into what we want Him to be at any given time. Therefore, when our frantic attempts to do so yield no results, we might choose to give up, feeling that it is too difficult to understand His ways.

It is true that God never changes—rather, God *is* change; He embodies change. His character is multi-faceted like a diamond cut into an immeasurable number of surfaces, each side reflecting its own unique color as the light illuminates it. As God reveals different facets of Himself, it appears to us as if He is changing. And He is. He is showing us more and more of Himself, allowing us to understand His nature in fuller and fuller measure. However, the total, complete picture and package of who our Lord is remains intact.

As God reveals more of Himself to us, He desires that we change in order to become more like Him. And He certainly gives us plenty of opportunity to change. God constantly desires that we grow and mature. He longs for us to develop strong roots and blossom in all of our fullness and beauty. He also knows that we can be resistant to change and that sometimes we might need some prompting.

Times of difficulty surely provide us with both the occasion and the motivation to change. Trials and testing refine us, shape us and mold us. Building character and developing spiritual maturity takes time, which is why we often find ourselves in those times of waiting. So while we are waiting, why not use that time productively?

At one point during our time of testing, I thought that we had reached the other side. Yet I was amazed at how quickly I reverted to some old habits and ways of thinking. For all the lessons I had so painstakingly learned, I found myself quickly moving on, anxious to forget the past. Then just as rapidly as we had emerged, we were plummeted right back into the pit. In my disappointment, I also realized that I was not yet ready. I had more learning and changing to do that could only be accomplished from that difficult place of longing and need.

I once read a story of how a silversmith knows when the process of purifying is complete. It is when he can see his own image in the silver. So is it any wonder that Malachi says, "And He shall sit as a refiner and purifier of silver." Malachi 3:3 (NKJ)

When Christ can look at us and see His own image, His work of purifying will be complete. But while the work is going on, Jesus, just like the silversmith, never takes His eyes off us. He sits transfixed, for if the time necessary for refining is exceeded even slightly, the silver will be damaged. God loves us and cares for us deeply during our times of refining and change.

Clearly, there are various areas in our lives that need purifying. It's okay to not attempt to tackle all of them at once. That is probably one of the easiest ways to fail. Better to choose one area to really focus on and see some success than to experience widespread disappointment.

In whatever area you choose to change, also know that you will experience resistance and temptation. It can be very tantalizing to make the wrong choices, which is why sin looks so inviting. I thought of this analogy one day while Doug and I were driving home from a Sunday dinner at one of our favorite restaurants.

I was so pleased with myself that I had chosen a salad rather than the pot roast sandwich—with mashed potatoes. Realizing that I felt satisfied without that full, heavy, I-need-to-go-put-on-sweatpants feeling, I quipped, "You know what? Eating food that is not very good for you is just like sin. It only tastes good in your mouth—on the way down. Once you swallow it and it has a chance to lie around in there for a little while—ugh!"

When your mouth starts watering at the desire of the pot roast sandwich, or the bacon double-cheeseburger, or whatever your area of temptation may be—think about how you'll feel in an hour or so. Once the digestion process starts, the pleasure is long gone. All you're left with is a bad taste in your mouth and a sick feeling in your gut.

Another problem that happens with sin is that it becomes so familiar to us, that we no longer even recognize it. Many years ago, we had the kitchen of our home repainted. It had been over ten years since the walls had a fresh coat, so we knew it needed repainting, but we had also gotten used to how it looked. Upon returning home from work one day, I noticed that the painter was almost finished. Taking a peek around, I concluded that it seemed nice; but it was white, and the walls had been white before. I wasn't sure it looked very different.

It was then that my eyes landed on the area that had not yet been completed—what was probably the worst section of all, near the heating vent, where it was dingy, dark and blackened by some furnace problems years prior. I then noticed the contrast with the freshly coated area. How embarrassing! Spying the paint can, I noted that the color was called Pure White. Immediately, I saw the parallel.

Sin builds up in us over time, slowly causing us to become dark and dingy. But we don't notice; we think we're okay. Until by God's grace, we come side by side with the Pure White Holy One. We see our ugliness and it brings us to our knees. Then the Master Painter finishes His work and covers over our dirty lives with a fresh coat of His purity. And our relationship with Him is fully restored.

God longs for our repentance and restoration. He calls us to "be holy as I am holy." However, the choice to change is entirely up to us. If we ask for His assistance and guidance, God is willing to help guide us on our journey. Think of it this way:

Imagine driving on a long trip. In the beginning, you're fully attentive and concentrating on following the correct route. You're alert to the surrounding traffic and keeping your car in the center of the lane. But what sometimes happens after several hours of driving? If you're not careful, you can lose your focus and go on autopilot, becoming too relaxed, perhaps a bit sleepy, and no longer paying close attention.

If you start to drift too far off course—BUHHHHH!!!!! Those little ridges carved into the roadway provide a sudden and loud reminder that something is amiss. I know this well as there have been several occasions where this unwelcome sound has abruptly filled the inside of our vehicle—followed quickly by the sound of Doug's voice.

"What are ya' doin'?!!"

We can think of those grooves and that horrendous sound as God's discipline and direction on our road of life. It wakes us up—physically on the highway and spiritually in our walk with God. If we remain alert and stay in our lane through regular times of prayer, worship, Bible study and more, we can avoid some of the noise and bumps along the way.

At times, we may experience dramatic and sudden changes in our lives. More often, change and growth happens slowly, often so subtly that unless we are very attentive, we are likely to miss it. How is it in March that flowers appear overnight and buds on trees emerge out of nowhere? Have you ever tried to catch the grass turning that awesome shade of spring green?

One year a friend and I were determined to see the grass change colors. Every day on the trip to and from work, we would carefully study the lawns, looking for any hint that the color was about to pop. Incredibly, we very nearly saw it, though the greatest change still seemed to occur overnight when we weren't looking.

Nevertheless, catching even a glimpse took effort, concentration and determination. It is the same way with our spiritual lives. So putting some methods in place can be very useful in helping to chart your progress.

Periodically recording events in a journal is an especially nice way to note where you have been. It can be very enlightening to look back and see that indeed, God has changed you in ways that you never would have imagined.

Obtaining feedback from fellow believers is also helpful, especially if it is someone you haven't seen in a while. That person can be a great resource since they're not with you every day. To them, it will seem as though you have blossomed overnight!

In whatever way you choose, know that God will honor your efforts to change. It always thrills me whenever someone tells me that he or she sincerely desires to seek God more fully and is looking to develop a deeper relationship with Him. I know that that person has just embarked on a journey that will change his or her life forever.

I was raised in a Christian home and come from a long line of believers on both sides of my family. Growing up in the church and always having had at least some understanding of God's love, I never really thought I had much of a testimony. I also never fully understood my need for a Savior. However, in 1997, I had a desire like never before to one day hear God say, "Well done, good and faithful servant." My life has been changing ever since. Sometimes quite rapidly and on other occasions, at a snail's pace, but the Lord has honored my prayer.

I also now realize that I have a tremendous testimony. I didn't need to be dramatically saved from a life of drugs or crime. It's okay that I never turned my back on God or needed an incredible, near-death event to transform my life. Those types of testimonies are awesome and speak to the amazing power, love and grace of God. And so does mine.

God has loved every one of us from before we were born. I just happened to love Him back earlier than some. I am thankful that I don't carry the burdens and baggage from a life lived far from God. But I am every bit as in need of His grace as one who does.

No matter your starting point—change is always possible. And it's exciting! "No eye has seen, no ear has heard, and no mind has imagined what God has prepared for those who love Him." 1 Corinthians 2:9 (NLT)

So join me on a journey of change this March. Thaw out the dark, hardened places of your heart; then start breaking up the fallow ground. For it's time to plant.

April: A time to plant

*"It's not important who does the **planting**, or who does the watering. What's important is that God makes the seed grow. The one who **plants** and the one who waters work together with the same purpose. And both will be rewarded for their own hard work. For we are both God's workers. And you are God's field. You are God's building."*

1 Corinthians 3:7-9 (NLT)

April is a beautiful time of year—it seems all of nature is preparing to birth new life. As we celebrate Easter and Jesus's miraculous resurrection, we are also witnesses to this wonder-filled month of renewal and regeneration. In this month, fields and gardens are planted, nests are built, and eggs are laid.

Jesus told many parables relating to seeds and planting which are necessary to produce crops and new life. A number of years ago, I was thrilled when God gave me my very own springtime parable.

It started the moment I discovered a bird's nest built in the wreath on the entrance to our home. A mother finch then carefully laid her eggs, and in due time, we had three baby finches on our front door. Every morning I would open the door and take a peek, watching them grow until the day they fluttered away.

The following spring, mom finch was back at work on her front door nest. But that wasn't all. Apparently, she had made an announcement about us through the bird network, because there were finches in the windows by the air conditioners, there was a dove up by the roof, and there was a pair of ducks in the backyard. I thought,

"Oh my goodness, we've started a bird sanctuary!" My observations of those feathered friends became my parable.

There was a pair of ducks—and they wanted to build their nest in the best possible place. They wandered and they searched diligently, night after night, combing the backyard for just the perfect spot. But they never found it. So they never built anything—and as a result—they produced nothing.

There was a pair of finches. They gave it their all! Husband and wife finch working heartily together to build the best nest they could. Sometimes they sang and sometimes it sounded like arguing, but they brought many substances—twigs, grass, all the right materials, everything they needed. But they put it all in the wrong place. Instead of building a nest, they put everything *under* the air conditioner. That space was stuffed full, but it was all useless—and as a result—they produced nothing.

There was a second pair of finches. They were building onto the nest from last year on the front door. They added a little bit here and a little bit there. Now and then, they would find a piece of a weed, or a little bit of tissue; scraps of this and that which they would periodically add in. But they never fully committed to building anything—and as a result—they produced nothing.

There was a dove. She had the best location of all—under the eave of the roof where she was well protected. She built the biggest nest. And she built it well. She used good materials and it was strong and sturdy. She sat on her nest proudly. Sometimes she would perch on the roof and sing about it. But as good as it looked, she never filled it with anything—and as a result—she produced nothing.

There was a third pair of finches. They worked hard. On occasion, they sang or were quite noisy; other times they just quietly went about their work. They made a nest in the upstairs window by the air conditioner. When I thought about it, I realized that they had been there other years as well. However, I never really noticed. Without much fuss, they carried out their task—and as a result—they produced something—baby birds.

Now let's go back through and take a closer look at this bevy of bird stories. Ponder if you are able to relate to any of these feathered creatures.

Are you a Backyard Duck? These people are searching for the perfect church, waiting for the ideal time, looking for the exact opportune moment to start serving God. For instance, "When the kids are grown, the mortgage is paid, and my schedule is freed up, I'm going to get serious about my faith." If you find yourself relating to this pair, please reflect on these thoughts.

There is no flawless church; there is no perfect time to start giving or serving. God would desire that you find a place to plant yourself so you can begin walking with Him more closely and caring for others. Your waiting is only producing more of nothing. God longs for you to settle in and start producing something of value right now.

Are you a Misguided Finch? These people work heartily and are very productive with their lives. However, they are putting all their time, effort, and money into things that will not last. Just like those birds who stuffed that opening full. You cannot imagine how much material we pulled out of there! The Bible talks about our works that will last into eternity versus those that have no permanent value. So please consider—where are you building? Is your hard work and all your effort going to be useful in the end? Are you sowing seed that will blossom and produce life-giving fruit?

Are you a Front Door Finch? These folks mean well, at least some of the time. However, they just never seem to make a full commitment. This is someone who periodically throws some loose change or a dollar or two into the offering plate when the collection is taken. Maybe once or twice a year he or she helps with some area of service at church. But the harsh truth is that God does not want our scraps! He does not want us just throwing in a little effort here and there. He desires fully devoted, committed followers who are going to build His church and produce lasting results for His glory.

Are you a For Show Only Dove? When God was giving me this parable and showing me the meanings of the different birds, I thought, "Wow, this is amazing, but it would have been awesome if the dove had been the one to lay the eggs," since she would represent the Christian. I said, "God, this is great but you kind of messed up— the dove should've been the one." He said, "You're right—the dove *should* have been the one—but she wasn't." And I got goosebumps!

As Christians, we should be the ones. We are the ones who should be fruitful. We are the ones who should be giving and serving, and pouring out our lives for one another. But are we? Or are we just sitting on our big, beautiful, protected nests, proudly admiring our surroundings and enjoying how we look to others? And we can sometimes fool each other. But God knows our hearts—and He is looking for hearts that are pure and holy and running hard after Him.

Lastly then, are you a Fruitful Finch? These people are serving God wholeheartedly to the best of their abilities. Folks who are giving their all—daily—in whatever areas God has called them to serve. People who plant, produce and blossom—quietly—without anyone even noticing, while they steadily carry out His work—year after year after year.

God wants us to be fruitful with our lives. He longs for us to use the talents, gifts and unique abilities that He has blessed each one of us with to expand His kingdom. The Lord smiles when we plant seeds in others' lives and when we allow the seeds that have been planted in us to grow and bloom.

May this verse be true of us as well as those whose lives we have touched: "The righteous will flourish like a palm tree, they will grow like a cedar of Lebanon; planted in the house of the Lord, they will flourish in the courts of our God. They will still bear fruit in old age, they will stay fresh and green...." Psalm 92:12-14 (NIV)

In order to produce a bountiful crop, we need to first sow the seeds. To a certain extent, I believe all of us are called to plant. However, some undoubtedly have more of a calling in this area than others. Over time, I have discovered that I am definitely a "planter." I am amazed and humbled by the variety of ways and opportunities that God has given me to impact an ever-widening group of people. Person by person, life by life, seed by seed.

Just once I would truly enjoy experiencing what it is like to "harvest" a soul for Christ, but I am comforted by these words of Jesus: "What joy awaits both the planter and the harvester alike! You know the saying, 'One plants and another harvests.' And it's true. I sent you to harvest where you didn't plant; others had already done the work, and now you will get to gather the harvest." John 4:36-38 (NLT)

We all have a role to play and joy awaits each one of us. The Lord appoints and anoints as He chooses and we should delight in our individual callings. So I will continue to plant and sow to the best of my abilities and I will rejoice greatly with those who have been chosen to harvest. Because in the end, we will celebrate together!

Living in the heart of Lancaster County, Pennsylvania, I have certainly seen my share of the countryside. And when the unmistakable scent of liquid manure is in the air, I know that the farmers are hard at work. The familiar odor is a sure sign that spring has arrived and it is time to plant.

I have often marveled at the perfectly straight rows of crops in the many fields dotting the landscape. No doubt, there are various mechanisms used to accomplish this task. I have heard that one technique is for the farmer to keep his eyes fixed on a fencepost at the end of the field. In the same way, we need to keep our focus on Jesus so that our planting lines up with His ways. Proverbs instructs us to "Look straight ahead, and fix your eyes on what lies before you. Mark out a straight path for your feet; stay on the safe path." Proverbs 4:25-26 (NLT)

God prepares the soil and He alone changes hearts. Yet He invites us to join in the process of planting seeds in the souls of others. Seeds of hope, encouragement, peace, salvation... The possibilities are as endless as the variety of crops. So plant as you are called and gifted. A soybean farmer doesn't plant corn. If God has blessed you with the ability to encourage others, sow your seeds of inspiration with great joy. Don't feel guilty that you're not sharing the message of salvation with everyone you meet. That might not be the crop you were chosen to plant.

In the same way, do not be concerned if others' fields are larger than yours are or if their crops appear taller. Keep your focus on how, when, where and what God has called you to plant. Rejoice with your fellow planter just as he or she should celebrate with you. Don't compare or keep track of who has planted more seeds. There is no need for jealousy in God's garden.

Also, keep in mind that while we are called to plant, God will provide the increase. He causes the crops to grow, and it is by His providence alone as to if and when our precious seeds will begin to sprout. We are not to worry or fret or attempt to take control over the seedlings. That is best left in the hands of the Master Gardener.

So as this beautiful month of April unfolds, plant in joy—plant in hope—plant in peace. And then it is time to trust.

May: A time to trust

*"For the word of the Lord holds true, and everything He does is worthy of our **trust**."* Psalm 33:4 (NLT)

The lovely month of May. Colorful flowers brighten the landscape, the sweet scent of newly mown grass fills the air and the soothing rays of sunshine bring warmth to our bodies and souls. The beauty of May can bring comfort and reassurance like no other month. It can also be a time to trust. Just as the farmer now waits for his crops to grow, we need to trust that the seeds planted in us or in others will yield a plentiful return in due time.

Ecclesiastes 11:4-5 (NLT) says, "Farmers who wait for perfect weather never plant. If they watch every cloud, they never harvest. Just as you cannot understand the path of the wind or the mystery of a tiny baby growing in its mother's womb, so you cannot understand the activity of God, who does all things."

Farming, perhaps more than any other occupation, is at the mercy of God's hand. These laborers have absolutely no control over the weather and how it may affect their season's crops. While they need to tend to their growing seeds, nourish their growth and minimize the threat of weeds, there is also a great measure of trust inherent in their work. There is only so much they can regulate. The rest is left to faith.

So it is with our spiritual lives. We can sow seeds, nurture growth in our own hearts and minds as well as the souls of others, but then comes the matter of trust. The time when we have done all we can and there is nothing left to do but stand. Stand tall and strong...and trust.

This is not easy. As with so many aspects of the journey of faith, trusting in the unseen can be difficult at best. When drought or floods come, when our tiny seeds of faith and hope are uprooted or choked by the troubles of life—worry and fear, rather than trust, tends to be our natural response.

It is during these times that we can take comfort in scriptures such as this one from Psalms. "Taste and see that the Lord is good. Oh, the joys of those who take refuge in Him! Fear the Lord you His godly people, for those who fear Him will have all they need. Even strong young lions sometimes go hungry, but those who trust in the Lord will lack no good thing." Psalm 34:8-10 (NLT)

I turned to the Psalms repeatedly when fear threatened to overwhelm me during those difficult years of my life. Feeling confused and helpless, I repeated Psalm 33 over and over, reminding myself of its truth—that indeed everything, EVERY THING the Lord does is worthy of my trust. Whether or not I understood what was happening at that time, agreed with it, or could wrap my mind around it, did not change the fact of this truth. If I was going to trust God with my circumstances, then I needed to trust Him fully. As our difficulties continued to mount, I was funneled and squeezed into an ever-narrowing channel where trusting became my only hope.

And God, in His own magnificent way, assured me of His promises. I began to notice a small rainbow on the passenger seat of my vehicle when I went out to my car during my lunch break at work. Nearly every day it was there, though I never determined how the likeness was made. So began my season of rainbows.

Almost daily, I would see a rainbow in one form or another. Sometimes it was an actual colored arch in the sky; on other occasions, it came in a wide assortment of variations. A logo on a passing truck, a kaleidoscopic beam streaming through a restaurant window, a circle of color ringed around a ceiling light, a sign advertising Rainbow vacuum cleaners, a picture on a greeting card or perhaps a shiny oil slick.

Driving home from work one rainy day, I was lamenting to God that I had not yet seen my daily symbol of promise. Just then, my eyes shifted to the headlights of the cars coming towards me. With each passing vehicle, two rows of color streamed down to the road. Rainbow, rainbow, rainbow... promise, promise, promise... trust, trust, trust...

These faithful symbols continued for over a year. One afternoon as I sat on my front porch admiring a gorgeous rainbow after a thunderstorm, I noticed that the rainbow was in the dark part of the sky. The promise is found in the darkness. Just as a rainbow is formed when the sun shines on falling rain, when we let the *Son* shine on our darkness, on our falling teardrops, we will shine. And we can bring hope to all who need courage to keep trusting.

While I was busy spotting rainbows, Doug had his own symbol of hope. On one of his darkest days of trying to get his business started, my husband felt completely alone. Questioning everything at that point, he even doubted his own salvation. Taking a cue from Gideon, he asked God to have some geese fly over his head when he took the garbage out later in the day if indeed, things were going to be okay.

By then forgetting about his "geese fleece," Doug was clearly startled when seven birds forming a perfect V flew directly over his head, honking loudly as they went, as he nonchalantly stepped out the back door, trash bag in hand. He said they were flying so low, he felt as though he could practically touch their feet!

And the geese continued to soar. For the next several years, geese would repeatedly fly overhead. While in our cars, separately or together, when we'd step out the back door, even while inside we'd hear them—honk, honk, honk…directly over the house. Large flocks, small flocks, spring, summer, fall, winter. The geese just kept flying.

Especially while driving, the number of times that a group of Canadian geese intersected with precision timing to soar directly over our cars simply defies logic. Yet there they were, time and time and time again.

Rainbows and geese—it was truly a journey of trust. Our God is so loving and caring. He longs to show Himself to us in an endless variety of ways. Yet too often, we are either too busy or perhaps too worried to notice. During difficult situations, our natural inclination is to worry. Which is probably why the Bible says, "Don't worry, don't worry, don't worry," in verse after verse after verse.

One of my favorite passages on worrying is from Matthew 6. After comparing God's care of the flowers and birds to His love for His followers, Jesus encourages them with these words. "But seek first His kingdom and His righteousness, and all these things will be given to you as well. Therefore do not worry about tomorrow, for tomorrow will worry about itself. Each day has enough trouble of its own." Matthew 6:33-34 (NIV)

Each day surely does have enough trouble of its own. We don't need to be fretting about yesterday and tomorrow; today is plenty enough to be concerned about. I believe "give us this day our daily bread" is an encouragement for us to take one day at a time. Or in some situations, one hour or one moment may be all we can manage.

Many years ago, my work situation was extremely stressful and when morning came, I longed for nothing more than to close my eyes and pull the covers over my head. Especially on Wednesdays, when I needed to face a tense, nerve-wracking afternoon meeting.

One technique that helped me was to realize that it wasn't necessary to waste my entire morning worrying about an event that didn't take place until after lunch. So instead, I took the day hour by hour. I ate breakfast in peace, savored my hot, soothing shower, and refreshed my soul with praise-filled music during the half-hour drive to the office. 1:30 came soon enough—I didn't need to ruin the rest of my Wednesday in anticipation of that one meeting.

God wants us to trust Him to meet our needs whether we take it daily, hourly, or minute by minute. He is never in a hurry.

But what happens when we believe we have trusted Him fully, taken that leap of faith, and instead of landing softly in the waiting, caring arms of our Father, we instead splatter on the sidewalk, battered and broken?

Some would say we did not trust fully enough. Others might think we leaped at the wrong time, in the wrong way, or out of the wrong window. Perhaps we are told that we actually were caught—it only *feels* like we have been splattered.

It is far beyond my capacity to comprehend even a glimpse of the mysterious dance between our choices, God's will, and life's circumstances. However, I do understand the hurt, confusion and pain of seeing all you believed to be true, lie crushed and broken, with hopes dashed and dreams destroyed.

What happens then? We gather the broken pieces of our shattered hearts and with reddened eyes and on bruised knees, we hold our trembling hands towards Heaven and ask in faith for Daddy to put the pieces together. We dare to trust again.

Several years ago, during a Sunday morning church service, we were given the opportunity to come forward, take a marker and write down on a piece of pottery, any hurt, sin, or difficulty—anything in our lives that we wanted to abolish. After placing the plate or cup into a Ziploc bag and a pillowcase, we then took a hammer and smashed it to bits. It was a liberating exercise in letting go of areas that were hindering our faith or causing grief or sorrow.

Unbeknownst to most of the congregation, we returned the next week to find an incredibly stunning mosaic picturing a cross and the bread and cup, on top of our communion table, made from pieces of the broken pottery. The gifted artisans from our body made sure to include at least one piece of stoneware from every person's bag.

What an incredible picture of God making something beautiful and new out of the damaged, shattered pieces of our lives. As a church body, it symbolizes our collective hearts—individually broken, yet joined together and made whole, each one representing a necessary piece of our communal life together.

Only God can make something beautiful and new from our splintered dreams and lost hopes. He can put the pieces of our broken hearts back together again. If only we let Him. If only we will dare to trust Him one more time. And one more time. And one more time. For as long as it takes.

Just as it takes time for the crops to grow after they are planted, so it is with our spiritual growth. God will bring the harvest in His timing and in His way. Our role is to keep believing that His ways are always best.

In what areas might God be calling you to continue trusting Him? Maybe you feel your heart has been broken and shattered beyond repair. Perhaps you're waiting for seeds of employment to develop. Or for a wayward son or daughter to return to their roots. Possibly you are wondering how long it will take for some medical issues to be weeded out of your path. God knows your longings and He feels your pain. Whether or not you can sense His presence, He is right there beside you in your garden of life.

So as the flowers of May reflect the glory of their Creator, let your beauty unfold under the loving hands of your Maker. Trust in

His care. Trust in His provision. Trust in His timing. As you do, your seeds of faith will grow and develop into a fully mature, beautiful, blossoming harvest. And what was once broken, will be made whole and new. Then from that place of growth and newfound hope—you'll find that it's time to give.

SUMMER

*"Both day and night belong to you; You made the starlight and the sun. You set the boundaries of the earth, and You made both **summer** and winter."* Psalm 74:16-18 (NLT)

Radiant sun beaming, hamburgers sizzling, fireflies dancing, children splashing... some of the sights and sounds of summer. As a child, it seemed as though the warm days and humid nights of summer stretched on endlessly. Lazy afternoons at the community pool, backyard games of kickball, and long evenings toasting marshmallows around a campfire with family and friends are just a few of my summertime memories.

As an adult, I have sadly learned that summer's nightfall comes much sooner than I remembered. A full-time job lessens the opportunity for daytime activities and I have become far less tolerant of the season's heat waves. Still, summer brings its own unique flavor that no other time of the year can equal.

Weddings, picnics, parties and vacations flourish during this season. Moreover, these three months can provide a time of relaxation and refreshment like none other when we slow down enough to enjoy them. If we can allow ourselves a break from the hectic pace of daily life for long enough—we just might catch a glimpse of childhood wonder.

So play with a puppy, relax on your front porch, take a long stroll with a friend, chase a lightening bug, throw your head back and laugh till your stomach hurts. For summer can be an occasion to give—a cause to celebrate—and it can bring an opportunity to rest.

These are the times of summer.

June: A time to give

*"You must each decide in your heart how much to **give**. And don't
give reluctantly or in response to pressure. For God loves a person
who **gives** cheerfully."* 2 Corinthians 9:7 (NLT)

School is over! As shouts of freedom ring out from students and
teachers alike, it's a certain sign that the month of June has
arrived. Some of us may not have a significant change in our
schedules, yet June somehow still evokes a feeling of being free.
Summer has officially begun and with it comes a wide variety of
events and activities.

It is a time to give gifts to the newly graduated, a time when
couples give themselves to each other in marriage, a time when
perhaps we give ourselves a chance to relax on a well-deserved
vacation. Giving comes in many different forms. It also carries with it
a variety of connotations, not all of which are positive—especially
when it comes to giving in the church.

Encouraging giving through guilt, pressure, intimidation or
false promises does little to inspire folks to part with their hard-earned
money or valuable time, resources and talents. God desires that we
give cheerfully, willingly, and literally, hilariously. Oh that we might
laugh uproariously as we give our offerings on a Sunday morning!

How can we arrive at such a place of freedom? Perhaps by
starting to understand in a deeper way that all we have has been freely
given to us by our Creator. Do we participate by using our talents and
gifts and working diligently for every dollar we earn? Absolutely! But
in that, we can also recognize that the gifts, talents and abilities to

work were first given to us by our loving Father. And if we use them for His glory and surrender all that we have and all that we are back to Him, then we might not grasp so tightly to the ownership of what we feel is rightfully ours.

This is certainly a struggle and an area that I, in no way, will claim to have mastered. But perhaps my experiences and thoughts can help others to find freedom.

Throughout our nearly thirty years of marriage, Doug and I have consistently given of our finances. However, I cannot say that I have always given cheerfully. For many years, it seemed as though we continually had just enough. Enough—but *just* enough. So over time, I became less thankful for God's provision and increasingly frustrated and angry with Him for not increasing our prosperity. Feeling unsatisfied, I became jealous of others' possessions and I began to wonder what the purpose was to all this giving. After all—isn't God supposed to bless our giving—and give us more? At that point, we had given faithfully for nearly fifteen years! What did we get? Just enough.

On one occasion, we had several large unexpected bills due at the same time, so we asked one of our church leaders to pray for us. Sincerely, he prayed that God would give us "just enough."

By then, I had had just about enough! At that time, I did not have a moment of humble surrender where I submissively turned everything over to God regarding my attitude toward our finances. I believe I was just plain angry! Yet something in my spirit had reached its limit and that seems to be the place where human frailty meets divine love and revelation can be given.

By my heavenly Father's loving grace, I realized that the issue was neither our finances nor God's response to our giving—it was my attitude. With a deeper understanding, I saw that I needed to relinquish control of our money, just as I had given up control in some other areas of my life. God showed me that all I had was His, including our money. It was never mine to begin with, so it was no wonder that I was unable to control it.

That understanding then brought me to a place of repentance after which I began to experience a peace and freedom in giving that I had never known before. We were blessed at that time with more income and we were able to give more than ever before.

"Give, and you will receive. Your gift will return to you in full—pressed down, shaken together to make room for more, running over, and poured into your lap. The amount you give will determine the amount you get back." Luke 6:38 (NLT)

This is an amazing promise and it sounds so simple. Yet the ongoing humble attitude required to give joyously and freely, not holding anything back and without any expectation as to the results, remains a challenge to me. Despite my newfound freedom in giving those many years ago, fully releasing ownership of money and possessions is an ongoing struggle for me.

I recently heard this story on the radio that simply astounded me. A woman called in to the station to share her experiences. She relayed how she was a single mom, already struggling to make ends meet, when she lost her job. Having only a few dollars left in her bank account, she withdrew the small amount of funds. She also gathered her children and told them to collect all the money they could find. They emptied their piggy banks, scoured the car, burrowed under the sofa cushions and gathered every bit of change they came across. They pooled all of their precious bills and coins and then she announced to her kids that tomorrow at church, they would place it all in the offering plate.

Telling no one of her circumstances, this dear soul wanted to show her children what it really meant to trust God. And if she was going to do that, she wanted to do it fully. Little happened during the next few weeks. But then her return began to come back to her in full measure. Her landlord offered her a free month's rent, food was provided, she was hired for a well-paying job...

Like the poor widow who dropped in two small coins at the Temple collection box, Jesus had to be pleased with this modern-day woman who also gave all she had. I have yet to know that level of trust in giving. What a tremendous freedom if we could unclench our fists long enough to surrender ourselves so completely to our loving Daddy.

I also recall hearing a very wealthy gentleman speak of how his attitude was the same regardless of how much or how little he had. Though he possessed millions, he lived in the reality that all he had belonged to God. Holding on to none of it, this faithful servant was blessed with more and more.

I am reminded of the rich man who asked Jesus what he must do to inherit eternal life. After assuring Jesus that he had been obeying all of the necessary commandments from childhood, Jesus offered him this challenge in love: "There is still one thing you haven't done," He told him. "Go and sell all your possessions and give the money to the poor, and you will have treasure in heaven. Then come, follow Me." At this the man's face fell, and he went away sad, for he had many possessions." Mark 10:21-22 (NLT)

Jesus wanted every part of that man, right then, right there. Even more than his wealth, Jesus desired this man's heart. It seems that the more we have, the more difficult it can be to surrender. This gentleman had much and he was unwilling and unable to part with his possessions. His belongings appeared to own him rather than him owning them.

I believe God is more concerned with our attitudes towards our assets than He is with our belongings themselves. As an example, let's consider a fellow named Bill who owns a brand new luxury

BMW. Bill absolutely loves this vehicle; he shines it up every day and insures that it is in perfect condition at all times. He enjoys seeing his neighbors' envy. Bill drives his car to work and uses it for errands. If necessary, he'll allow his kids in it—but their shoes had better be clean because if muddy feet get inside that car…! Bill also needs his car to remain in a pristine state since he is planning to trade up in two years—and then he'll truly be happy.

Now let's look at John. This man owns the exact same model BMW. John takes good care of his vehicle; he needs to because he plans to keep it for the next ten years. John also uses his car for work and errands. And if the kids track some dirt in—there's always carpet cleaner.

John has an elderly neighbor who can't drive anymore, so John sometimes takes her to the pharmacy to get her medication. He also has a friend who wants to attend church but is uncomfortable going on his own for the first time. So John uses his BMW to pick up his friend and bring him along to the service. When another neighbor's car breaks down and the family is without transportation for a few days, John lends them his vehicle until they can get theirs fixed.

"For the love of money is the root of all kinds of evil." 1 Timothy 6:10 (NLT) It's not what we own or how much we own. It's what we do with what we have that matters.

In thinking about what it means to give, I thought of this simple definition—Gladly I Volunteer Everything. Our giving needs to come from a grateful heart so we can give of our possessions and ourselves gladly, joyfully, cheerfully and hilariously.

Our attitude in giving, as well as how much or how little we give, is an individual decision. We are each responsible for the choices we make in this area as well as the consequences of those choices. In a marriage, we would hopefully consult with our spouse and come to a mutual agreement as to financial decisions. Yet there remains some individual responsibility in making God-honoring choices.

Giving, as well as any other aspect of the Christian walk of faith, is voluntary. If God had not given us the ability to freely make our own decisions, we would be little more than puppets. God longs for us to love Him in return, but His love towards us does not change no matter what we decide. He will not love us more nor will He love us less.

Think of the delight that is felt by both parties when we voluntarily and unexpectedly offer a gift to a friend. How much greater is the joy than when a gift is given out of compulsion or requirement.

So too, when we gladly volunteer to surrender everything to God, we can experience a freedom that will change our lives forever. My aim is to know that complete freedom myself. The freedom to give, the freedom to serve, the freedom to love; expecting nothing in return, but only doing so out of a heart overflowing with the love of Christ for those He loved first.

If we can catch even a glimpse of that kind of giving and that kind of love—then as we journey through summer from June into July—it will surely be time to celebrate!

July: A time to celebrate

*"People of all nations, **celebrate** God! All colors and races, give hearty praise!"* Romans 15:11 (MSG)

Fireworks, picnics, parties and fun—July is here and it's time to celebrate! So run barefoot through the grass, take a splash in a swimming pool, set off a firecracker and let the watermelon juice run down your chin. Return to the joys of your childhood, if only for an afternoon.

Age seems to have a way of diminishing our joy. As career, family and health concerns mount, times of laughter and fun become far too scarce. William Fry and Patch Adams, both known for their research on humor, state that children laugh about 400 times a day while adults average 17 times.

Even more sadly, many folks believe that in order to be a true follower of Christ, a somber and serious spirit is a strict requirement. Yet Jesus rebuked the disciples for shooing away the little ones saying, "Let the children come to me. Don't stop them! For the Kingdom of Heaven belongs to those who are like these children." Matthew 19:14 (NLT)

If we need to be as children to enter God's glory, then I would imagine it is quite acceptable to laugh now and then. Also of note is the contrast between childlike and childish. This is an important difference and one that is also noted in Scripture. We are told to "put away childish things" and to "not be childish in our understanding."

Being childish involves immaturity and self-indulgence. Child-likeness, in comparison, evokes images of innocence, expectation and simple trust. Along with copious amounts of laughter and joy!

Seeing a toddler experience the wonder of a world never before seen is a remarkable sight. We may wish that we could step back in time and share his or her vision of innocence. But alas, we've already seen it all.

Or have we? Have we already beheld every color and variation ever created in God's glorious daily sunrise and sunset? Have we fully comprehended the magnificence of each sea creature in the ocean's depths? Can we truly ever tire of viewing the sky's incredible shade of blue on a cloudless summer day? Opportunities for joy and wonder abound if only we would take the time to celebrate them.

The seriousness and stressors of life will not disappear. However, perhaps the power they have over us can be mediated somewhat if we are intentional in seeking joy and laughter instead of only focusing on our worries and cares.

So spend some time with children and giggle along with them on their way to 400. Watch a funny movie with friends or family. Laughing in a group is always more enjoyable than when alone—for laughter is contagious, especially when you're with someone with a really great laugh. After a time, you end up in hysterics and can't even remember what was so funny to begin with.

Have you ever seen the portrait of the "Laughing Jesus?" With head cocked back, eyes dancing and mouth agape, He invites us to chortle along with Him. Contrast that with the depictions of Jesus as a gaunt, pale, hollow-eyed, lifeless soul. Obviously, our Lord had an intense, serious side as He walked this earth. But I refuse to believe that He didn't also possess a most hearty laugh that delighted all those who crossed His path.

We can still take delight in laughing with Him today. God's sense of humor is readily apparent to those who are looking for it.

One evening a number of years ago, I felt called to begin journaling again. In my frustration over our years of difficulties, I had stopped putting my feelings on paper. That evening, I felt a strong calling to watch a reality show on television. Yet an even greater urge beckoned me to prayer and a notebook. Grabbing a unique-looking pen that I found in our pencil holder, I settled in to listen. God reassured me in a beautiful way that He loved me and that my heart belonged to Him. Finishing my "love letter" to my Beloved, I walked across the living room and returned the pen to its holder.

About ten minutes later, Doug returned home and I told him about my special time with God. Standing up, I saw something fall from the blanket that I had wrapped around me. In amazement, I saw that it was a pen that looked identical to the one I had just been using. Knowing that I had already put the original pen away, I double-checked that it was still in its place across the room. Having no idea where the second pen came from, I took it as a symbol that God would multiply and bless us in the future, perhaps with a double portion.

Telling a friend about the story the next night, she exclaimed, "I think He wants you to write!"

"I don't write!" I told her in protest. "I hardly even read." Books had never held much fascination for me and other than occasional journaling, I had never had any interest in writing.

Now nearly seven years later, here I sit writing this, my second book. I am also seeking a publisher for a children's story that dropped into my mind one morning as unexpectedly as that pen dropped out of my blanket. God's humor is evident. He was laughing then and He is laughing now. And I am laughing with Him.

Who better to share a joke with than the inventor of humor Himself? God longs for us to laugh with Him. Even in church.

Some years ago, before I presented a message on God's fun, our worship pastor helped to prepare the mood of the congregation. There were some humorous stories told and some other antics, but my favorite was when he led the group in "the wave." Perhaps not as grand as in a sports stadium, but as shouts of "Ohhhhhh!!" rang out as we stood and raised our arms, going across the auditorium and then back again, it most certainly lightened the atmosphere in the room.

Our church body has had many, many serious, solemn and somber moments, but we also know how to celebrate! There are times on a Sunday morning when we laugh until our sides hurt. And we feel God's joyous presence, reveling along with us.

There are some who might find that irreverent or sacrilegious. But didn't the father of the lost prodigal host a huge barbeque party to celebrate the return of his beloved son? We serve the same God who rejoices over every lost sheep who is found and brought back into the fold. Or who said of the woman who had diligently scoured her house in search of a lost coin, "'Celebrate with me! I found my lost coin!' Count on it—that's the kind of party God's angels throw every time one lost soul turns to God." Luke 15:9-10 (MSG)

There is a HUGE party coming at the end of the age where we will celebrate and enjoy a feast like none other! Where every tribe, tongue and nation will come together in glorious triumph to worship and behold the Lamb of God. So why wait until then to celebrate?

We can prepare for that day by practicing now. By laughing now, rejoicing now, and celebrating now. Now! We don't have to wait until the "sweet bye and bye" to be able to smile. It is not our lot in life to merely survive the miserable mess of this earth until Christ calls us home to Him. We are already free! Free from sin's grasp, free from any and all obstacles that would hold us back. So why live as if we are still chained and in bondage?

God longs for us to live in Heaven while we are still on earth. What better way to demonstrate His love to those who have not yet chosen Him? What a powerful witness the church could be by demonstrating love, compassion and understanding towards each other, rather than fighting over doctrinal differences. When barriers of age, race and gender are torn down and actions of care, acceptance, and tolerance are demonstrated instead, the world will stand up and take notice.

Just as each person has been gifted uniquely to contribute his or her talents and gifts, each church body can fulfill a distinct role in the body of Christ at large. So as churches, let's work together rather than tear each other down. My church understands that most congregations are not going to practice "the wave" during a Sunday morning service. That's part of the special flavor of our body. We only ask that we be respected for who we are just as we respect those churches with more traditional styles of worship.

Let's make a determined effort to celebrate our differences rather than condemn them. The differences are what make individuals and churches special. There is such beauty in diversity. How dull if we all looked alike!

There is plenty of fighting in our world. What better opportunity than within the church to show peace and kindness towards one another? Pulling down walls of judgment and prejudice is certainly no easy task. Yet the recognition of the need for this is at least a place to start.

1 Corinthians 12:12 says, "Some of us are Jews, some are Gentiles, some are slaves and some are free. But we have all been

baptized into Christ's body by one Spirit, and we have all received the same Spirit." (NLT)

Couldn't we just as easily say, "Some of us are Methodists, some are independents, some are Catholics and some are Baptists? But we have ALL been baptized into Christ's body by ONE Spirit, and we have ALL received the SAME Spirit."

In Christ, we are ONE. One Spirit, one body, one church. Each with our unique gifts and contributions, but one body working together in perfect harmony to reflect the power and glory of the one God we collectively worship. Now that is something to celebrate!

If we could become one, the world might truly "know we are Christians by our love." Not because the song lyrics say so. But because they see it lived out in front of them day after day after day. Let's come together as one in the worship of our Holy God.

The Bible also teaches us to encourage each other, no matter in what season we may find ourselves. "Rejoice with those who rejoice; mourn with those who mourn." Romans 12:15 (NIV)

Sometimes it might be difficult to feel celebratory if we are grieving. Yet it is all part of the body of Christ loving and caring for each other. Let's not allow resentment or envy to dampen our enthusiasm for rejoicing with those who are bursting with joy. Likewise, if we are in a time of triumph, we need to be mindful to remain compassionate and kind towards those who are hurting.

This July—as we celebrate our historical freedom on Independence Day—let us also celebrate the freedom we have in Christ. The freedom to love one another as God first loved us. The freedom to support and uphold one another as the Spirit helps bear our burdens. The freedom to intercede for one another as Jesus intercedes for us.

We are free to celebrate! Free to enjoy fellowship with one another. Free to enjoy God's creation. Free to laugh heartily. Free to relax—and perhaps even to enjoy a time of rest.

August: A time to rest

*"It is useless for you to work so hard from early morning until late at night, anxiously working for food to eat; for God gives **rest** to his loved ones."* Psalm 127:2 (NLT)

Ahhh, yes—the lazy dog days of August. Many of summer's busy activities are past and school is not yet started. What better time to grab a tall glass of ice-cold lemonade, sit out back under a shade tree with a good book and take a well-deserved rest.

"Rest?" you might be thinking, "How can I rest? My work schedule is crazy, the kids need back-to-school clothes, the dog needs to go to the vet, the flowerbed is full of weeds and the spring housecleaning never even got started. I can't rest!"

As an overworked, overscheduled, overextended, overtasked, overtaxed, sleep-deprived society, resting has become a lost art. There are simply not enough hours in the day to accomplish all that needs to be done and the thought of trying to schedule in a time to rest on top of everything else is quite simply impossible. So we keep pushing, keep pressing and keep demanding more and more of our minds and bodies until we finally crumble in exhaustion or illness. Even then, some folks persist in striving because they just don't know any other way.

Deep breath. It's okay to rest. Let me repeat that. It is OKAY to rest. I know this well because I probably have at least a master's degree in rest. Napping is most certainly among the list of my favorite activities. If anything, I could probably stand to be a bit more productive.

I have always enjoyed sleeping. I generally fall asleep quite easily and for the most part am still slumbering when my alarm goes off. I am neither a morning person nor a night person. My preference is to go to bed early and get up late. If I'm sick, I enjoy sleeping. If I'm happy, I enjoy sleeping. If I'm stressed, I enjoy sleeping. Even during the most difficult of circumstances, I have slept well and on occasion have awakened with the thought, "Is everything going okay right now or is there something I should be worrying about?"

During work, I often take my lunch break by a small pond close to the office. I enjoy watching the ducks and geese and it's a nice place to relax in the middle of a hectic day. On one occasion, I decided to recline the seat of my car and take a small nap. Having no alarm clock, I asked God to please wake me at 12:50 so I could return to the office by 1:00. Seemingly moments later, I was startled out of a sound sleep by three large male mallards standing directly by my driver's side window, quacking as loudly as their little duck throats could holler. I said, "Oh—the Father, Son and Holy Spirit. Thank you God." The clock read 12:50.

I am exceedingly grateful for this gift of rest and fully realize that peaceful slumber does not come so easily to everyone. However, please know that God longs for you to be at rest when nighttime falls. "When you lie down, you will not be afraid; when you lie down, your sleep will be sweet." Proverbs 3:24 (NIV)

God designed sleep to refresh and renew our bodies, minds and souls. He longs for us to slumber peacefully so we can start fresh the next day. A good night's rest can bring a new perspective on problems and perhaps the realization that feverish fretting and sleepless nights do little to resolve our concerns. Far more helpful is laying our burdens at the feet of Jesus.

This takes determination and discipline, but with continued practice, it can become more and more of a natural response.

Physically opening your hands in prayer may help to symbolize the release of your cares and worries. They are no longer yours to keep. Once you have sincerely turned your concerns over to your Father, they now rest with Him.

The moment those burdens start knocking again on your heart's door, know that you do not have to open it. All of the questions and "what if's" will only lead back to worry. They will never lead to rest. So cut them off the instant they appear with a strong declaration that God is handling those concerns now and you are trusting Him with them. You're trusting Him, you're trusting Him, you're trusting Him.

"He will take delight in you with gladness. With His love, He will calm all your fears. He will rejoice over you with joyful songs." Zephaniah 3:17 (NLT)

I absolutely love the fact that God sings over us! I imagine He is singing day and night, but I especially like the thought of His melodies washing over me while I sleep. Like a tender parent softly intoning a lullaby over a sleeping baby is our Lord gently rocking us to sleep with His sweet hymns of love.

God never slumbers nor sleeps. He is continually aware of our comings and goings. He is with us always—guiding, protecting, watching, waiting. Like the shepherd who keeps a constant vigil on his sheep, our Good Shepherd never lets His lambs out of sight. We can rest—for we are in His perfect care.

If we can learn to rest not just physically, but also mentally and emotionally, how much greater our peace will be. Psalm 46:10 says, "Be still, and know that I am God!" (NLT) But how can we practice stillness in the midst of our busy, busy lives? Obviously one way is to attempt to actually set aside some time to just sit quietly before God with as little distraction as possible. This may sound impractical and unachievable, but if you continue to make the effort, God will honor your time before Him.

Start by finding a few quiet moments in your day to just sit with Jesus. Perhaps with your Bible or a journal, or maybe just silently in prayer. Listening to a quiet worship song first may help to ready and calm your spirit. From there, you are free to enjoy His presence. It may feel awkward at first, but as with any spiritual exercise, you will become more comfortable over time.

Once you have learned how to practice stillness, you can be still even in the midst of chaos. When a friend is in crisis, you can be still. When your boss makes unreasonable demands, you can be still. When everything in you wants to scream at your defiant teenager, you can be still.

The practice of stillness brings peace. Not just when sitting quietly in those private moments with God. But in any situation, at any time, you can be calm and at rest in your spirit. And your stillness will radiate that peace, bringing comfort and calmness to those around you as well.

Stillness and peace of mind and spirit is also developed as a result of being content. In our hectic, fast-paced society, more is better and bigger is best. Whether it's yearning for a larger home, a more prestigious job, newer furniture or a fancier wardrobe, it seems as though we are always in a state of want.

I want… and if only… "If only I had more money; if only my kids didn't fight all the time; if only my spouse were more understanding; if only I didn't have all these health problems. Then I would be content. Then I'd be at peace."

If you find yourself continually striving and in a state of want, you will never know true rest.

In spite of all Doug and I had been through and how far God had brought us, in recent years I still found myself wanting and

wishing for more. Not a completely improper desire, because I truly
believe God does have greater things in store for us. Yet what was
brewing in my gut was not so much a holy longing, but instead a
growing discontent. Feeling increasingly dissatisfied and resentful, I
found myself becoming more easily irritated and short-tempered.

I was tired of seeing so much of my hard-earned paycheck
going towards the seemingly bottomless pit of debt we had accrued. I
wanted a place of our own again rather than continuing to rent. I
longed for new carpet and bigger closets. I grew weary of scraping
the ice off my windshield in the winter. "Can't I please just have a
garage?!"

Then one day by God's magnificent grace, I realized that my
silent longings were not at all productive. They could do nothing to
change our current situation; they were influencing my mood and my
attitude, and they were detrimental to my relationship with Doug.

So I took a step back and seriously considered my
circumstances. Despite still having some debt to pay off, our financial
situation was steadily improving. Our landlady had completed
numerous renovations to the property and had not raised our rent once
in the eight years we had been living in her home. We resided on a
wonderfully quiet street with kind and considerate neighbors. Those
were just a few of my blessings.

Perhaps, I thought, things were not so awful after all. Almost
immediately, I could feel a sense of stillness and peace wash over me.
Not one area in my outward circumstances had changed. But I felt a
level of joy that I had not known in years. I was content once again.
And with contentment came stillness and peace. And rest.

May I be able to say with Paul, "I have learned how to be
content with whatever I have. I know how to live on almost nothing or
with everything. I have learned the secret of living in every situation,
whether it is with a full stomach or empty, with plenty or little. For I

can do everything through Christ, who gives me strength." Philippians 4:11-13 (NLT)

Contrary to what we might like to believe, it also seems that contentment is easier to find when we have less, rather than more. Despite our constant striving for bigger, better, faster—more prestige, more possessions and more wealth only seems to bring more stress.

While winning the lottery may seem like a "dream come true," many winners have experienced quite the opposite. Some statistics state that up to 75% of multi-million dollar victors are broke within a few short years. There are most likely numerous reasons for this, but surely among them has to be the added complexity that riches bring.

The more complex our lives become, the greater our level of stress and the more difficult it is to find rest. An overabundance of "stuff" can easily steal our peace.

But how can we adopt a simpler lifestyle in a stressful, chaotic and frenetic-paced world? Learning to say no may be one place to start. It sounds so simple, yet saying that small two-letter word is extraordinarily difficult for many folks. For me, this comes fairly easily. "No." I can repeat it for you if necessary. "No."

"No" does not need to be spoken rudely or inconsiderately. It does not indicate incompetence or unfairness. It is not an indicator of reputation or character. Saying no is purely a matter of prioritizing and setting boundaries based on individual circumstances. Establishing limits and then keeping them is vital if you ever hope to acquire a less complicated way of life.

This will take great courage if you are someone who usually answers affirmatively. Maybe you truly want to complete the task; in other cases, your "yes" may be spoken out of a sense of duty, guilt or obligation. Perhaps you're afraid that the other person will be angry with you or think less of you. All of these scenarios need to be carefully considered. Then feel free to make a wise decision with care and concern for all involved, including your own needs.

Saying no as necessary is not being selfish. It is simply a way of protecting your precious and valuable time for yourself and your loved ones. It is a route to stillness and relaxation. It is a path to peace. It is an avenue to rest.

Learning to rest well is vital to our physical, emotional and spiritual health. From a place of rest, we will have more energy to love and serve others. When rested, we will be better equipped to withstand the turbulence of life's difficulties. In rest, we can more easily hear the sweet, quiet voice of our loving Father.

So take some time to rest this August. Conserve your energy—for autumn is coming—and it will soon be time to harvest.

AUTUMN

*"The God who gives rain in both spring and **autumn** and maintains the rhythm of the seasons."* Jeremiah 5:24 (MSG)

Trees ablaze in colors of red, orange and gold, a crispness in the night air, hot apple cider, marching bands trumpeting their teams on to victory… some of the sights and sounds of autumn.

Fall is a lovely time of year as crops are gathered, pumpkins are carved and Thanksgiving's bounty awaits. Autumn's coolness is a welcome relief from summer's heat and humidity, and golden light streaming down through brilliantly colored foliage brings beauty beyond compare.

Autumn brings an appreciation of both endings and beginnings. As the year is winding down, it's a time to gather and reap what was sown throughout the prior months. Autumn also brings a feeling of newness as regular routines resume and another school year begins. We are transported back to the simple pleasures of a brand-new pair of shoes and the anticipation of what lies ahead in this new season.

So as the leaves fall and the grasses wither, rake together the blessings you have gleaned during the past year. As the golden glow of an October moon shines down upon you, imagine what is yet to come. As you gather round with friends and family, let your heart swell with gratefulness. For autumn is the time to harvest—it is a reason to believe—and it is most certainly an occasion to thank.

These are the times of autumn.

September: A time to harvest

*"Those who plant in tears will **harvest** with shouts of joy. They weep as they go to plant their seed, but they sing as they return with the **harvest**."* Psalm 126:5-6 (NLT)

Although I haven't been in a classroom for nearly thirty years, my thoughts of September still seem to begin with "back-to-school." Followed closely by the vision of gorgeous-colored leaves and of course, the ever important question, "Are you ready for some football?"

I grew up watching the game and it is definitely a favorite family sport, especially on my father's side. There was never any difficulty in locating my paternal grandmother's room at the retirement community on a Sunday afternoon. Just follow the sound of the blaring football game broadcast and one was sure to find the nonagenarian's living space.

Yet certainly there is more to September than school, leaves and football. Yes—September is also the month for harvesting. A time to reap all that has been planted and sown previously.

For farmers, the harvest marks the end of the growing season, when the mature crops are gathered from the fields. It would follow then, that spiritual harvesting and reaping comes after a period of growing and maturing. And just as each crop has its own growth cycle, so too do the spiritual aspects of our lives.

Only the Lord of the harvest knows when we have developed fully enough to produce a fruitful yield. "So let's not get tired of doing what is good. At just the right time we will reap a harvest of blessing if we don't give up." Galatians 6:9 (NLT)

Truly, God is awe-inspiring for His always-perfect timing in the rhythm of our lives. I am overjoyed that my season of harvest appears to have finally begun.

My bond with Doug is stronger than ever. Work relationships are the most stress-free they have ever been in my twenty-one years in that environment. This unexpected venture into writing has enabled me to form friendships with folks I would never have met otherwise. Moreover, I am incredibly humbled by how God has touched others' lives through the words He has given me to speak and write.

I am busier than ever these days! I had always thought of the harvest as the time when you sat back and enjoyed the fruits of your labor. However, I have learned that on smaller farms, harvesting is the most labor-intensive activity of the growing season. Apparently, so it is with our spiritual times of harvest as well.

Although my life is now faster-paced than my rest-oriented personality might prefer, I am greatly enjoying the challenges and joys of this new season. Perhaps the promise given me so many years ago is starting to be realized.

At the height of our most difficult times, a woman at church pulled me aside one Sunday morning. "I think I'm supposed to pray for you," she said. Knowing nothing of our situation, but by God's prophetic gifting, Lisa spoke into my life in a most beautiful way. Among her encouraging words were that the Lord saw all that I had been through and knew all that I had sacrificed over the years. She spoke of how He will restore and rebuild and then emphatically, she declared, "In this life, in THIS life!"

Those assurances—coming straight from the throne room, through Lisa, and into my aching heart—held me together in some of my darkest days. Now I can sing with delight at God's sweet redemption. And just as He caught my every tear—He now joins me as I dance in celebration.

"Sown in sorrow, reaped in joy" surely represents my life.

Dealing with darkness and difficulties for so long taught me well how to endure hardship and pain. Yet during some brief respites when it seemed our circumstances were improving, I discovered that my tendency was to then turn away from God. Not that I ever stopped loving Him. Rather, it was a sense of, "Thanks for being with me during the challenging times. I think I'm okay to carry on by myself now. I'll call if I need You."

I am thankful that God continued to teach and train me, as it was not yet my time for the harvest. My prayer then became, "Lord, please let our situation be more positive again. Allow me more opportunities to practice learning how to love You well in the good times too."

Though scripture teaches us general principles and gives vital guidance on every aspect of our lives, there is no specific formula to follow. Times of harvesting, just as all other times and seasons, are by God's providence alone. I am relating my journey. Yours will be different, and well it should. For we are all unique—in personality, in gifting, in circumstances, and in experiences. While there may be similarities, the music of our life-songs will vary. But what a glorious symphony we create when we are all in tune with the One who conducts the orchestra.

In addition, may I always remember that any and all bounty reaped during my time of harvest belongs to Christ and is to be used for His glory. Let me never forget that it is only by His strength and by His grace that I may fulfill the purposes and plans that He has for me.

I have many capabilities as a result of the natural talents God has granted me. Though He has also chosen to gift me with an aptitude for writing, it does not come easily. Only by the Holy Spirit flowing through my heart and mind, can I create life-giving words for others to read. May God receive all the glory and praise due His name for all who are blessed through this book.

May we all find the purposes for which we were created and have the courage and tenacity to press on to achieve all that God has intended. Let the soil of our hearts be fertile ground when the seeds are sown, so that we may exemplify this group in Luke's parable: "And the seeds that fell on the good soil represent honest, good-hearted people who hear God's word, cling to it, and patiently produce a huge harvest." Luke 8:15 (NLT)

Our harvests will come at different times and in different ways. Yet God longs for us all to reap the bountiful blessings that He has planned for us.

So how can we produce a substantial harvest?

Luke 8 shows us that bringing forth a large harvest takes time. We need to stay on course even when it seems as though little is happening. There were so many times when I just wanted to give up as the struggles threatened to overwhelm me. Then I would remember Lisa's life-giving words and I would remind God of them. "In this life—in THIS life…" And I found the courage to carry on.

Over five years ago, during one of my journaling sessions, I was pouring out my hurt and frustrations in a letter to the Lord. I then allowed my hand to write freely what it seemed my loving Father was saying back to me. "I have great things in store for you. Things you won't believe," I penned.

These many years I have been very curious as to the meaning of those words, but trusted they were true. Only God knows what else He has planned, but becoming an author would truly be among "things I wouldn't believe."

If you are careworn and weary and your patience is wearing thin—persevere and persist. Cling to God's word—both His Biblical words and His individual words given to you by whatever means He conveyed them. Pray and trust—for your harvest is coming.

Our harvest, in part, is dependent upon how we use the resources, gifts and talents that have been entrusted to us. If we are stingy and greedy with what we give out, our return will yield little. The Bible states it simply: "You will always harvest what you plant." Galatians 6:7 (NLT)

This is not to invoke guilt or to promote self-indulgence. We are not to give much for the express purpose of receiving a large bounty in return. Always remember that God considers not just the amount given, but the intentions and state of one's heart as well.

Giving, with no strings attached, allows us the freedom to let go of the results. We are generous for no other reason than because God has been generous to us. We give because Christ first gave to us. We offer grace to others because grace has been given to us. Our harvest is coming.

How do we produce a fruitful yield? "Plant the good seeds of righteousness, and you will harvest a crop of love. Plow up the hard ground of your hearts, for now is the time to seek the Lord, that He may come and shower righteousness upon you." Hosea 10:12 (NLT)

After the spiritual seeds have been sown, we need to nurture them by seeking God. Without watering and fertilizing, seeds planted in the earth will wither and die. Our spirits will also grow dry and brittle without the refreshing rain of the Holy Spirit. This is especially important during the growing season. So cultivate the seedlings deep within your heart. Soak them with prayer and praise. Nurture them with sound Biblical teaching.

Hopefully we never stop developing and learning spiritually, but there are most certainly times in our lives when we are more clearly in a growing phase. Seeking God during these times is vital if we desire to produce a harvest.

When I fully yielded myself to God in 1997, my growing stage began almost immediately. What looked like roadblocks, barriers and setbacks were all part of the teaching and training that He used to help me mature.

More than anything else, I believe my role was and is to be a willing vessel—to continue to cooperate and be faithful as He leads me. Friends have told me I am both simple and profound. I do not possess the knowledge of many scholars—but I know the One who first knew me. I may not have the ability to interpret the book of Revelation—but I understand the meaning of a rainbow set in the sky. I might not be able to explain all the truths of Scripture—but I can describe the certainty within my soul.

I love God with all my heart. By His miraculous grace, He has done great things in me. He is doing great things through me. And He will give great things back to me. My harvest is coming. My harvest is here.

This September, may you too know a full, abundant and overflowing harvest. And if you are not yet reaping—then it's time to believe.

October: A time to believe

*"You are my servant. You have been chosen to know me, **believe** in me, and understand that I alone am God. There is no other God—there never has been, and there never will be."* Isaiah 43:10 (NLT)

As the air grows cooler and scarecrows, hay bales, mums and pumpkins begin to adorn yards and homes, it's evident that October has arrived. While an occasional "Indian summer" day may bless us with extra warmth—sweaters, jackets and blankets soon become the norm as we continue to move through autumn.

With fall schedules underway and the busy holiday season not yet upon us, October can be an opportune time to take stock. We may need to consider our physical provisions and insure that we are prepared for the coming winter. Spiritually, we can also reflect on our experiences during the past year and anticipate what is yet to come. But no matter where we have been or where we may be going, faith and belief are vital to our journeys.

As Charles Schulz's Linus held unswervingly to his conviction that the Great Pumpkin would appear, we need to hold fast to the belief in our unseen, yet ever-present God. And what a comfort to know that our loving Father has chosen us to believe in Him. Long before we were ever conceived, our Lord saw us, chose us and desired for us to love Him in return.

God loves us unconditionally. He adores us even when we disappoint Him. He treasures us even though we sin. He believes in us even if we doubt Him. Therefore, we can believe and trust God even during the times when He seems very far away. On one of my most difficult days, I began to cry almost immediately upon getting in my car to drive home from work.

As my cries turned to sobs and my heart felt broken beyond repair, a song came on the radio that I had never heard before. As the music and lyrics of Steven Curtis Chapman's "Believe Me Now" started to fill the inside of my vehicle, it also began to penetrate my throbbing soul.

Turning the volume up to drown out my wails, the Holy Spirit's presence washed over me. I felt God asking, "Will you believe me now? NOW. In the center of your sorrow, in the depths of your despair, can you trust that I am still God? I have never forsaken you and I never will. Believe me right here, right now. Believe me now."

That was one of the most powerful spiritual encounters of my life. Once again, when I needed Him most, God poured forth His love and grace.

His grace and mercy are with us always. On my frequent walks through our neighborhood, a parked tractor-trailer truck with the word "Grace" on it always comforted me. Though it was in reference to a company, the name carried far greater significance for me.

One day as I drove past the parking lot, I quickly glanced to my right and said out loud, "Oh no—no more grace!" as the familiar vehicle was nowhere in sight. A few days later, as I happened by on a leisurely walk, I was able to take a closer look. Another trailer had been parked right next to it, obscuring the view of my favorite truck. My "Grace-truck" was still there, right where it had always been.

Even when God's grace is obscured and His mercy is hidden, we can still believe that it is there. For it is. Sometimes we just need to slow down enough to notice. Don't despair if you can't readily see

God's hand in your circumstances. Know that His tender mercy and loving kindness is always present. His grace will never leave you.

While it is vital that we believe in God and trust Him fully, we also need to believe in ourselves. Our Lord longs for us to comprehend the value and worth we hold in His eyes. We are holy and precious in His sight, and in Christ we have great purpose. "For I know the plans I have for you," declares the Lord, "plans to prosper you and not to harm you, plans to give you hope and a future." Jeremiah 29:11 (NIV)

We serve an amazing God and He has marvelous and beautiful dreams designed specifically for each one of us. So dream big! Hope greatly! Believe immensely! For God believes in you. "Now all glory to God, who is able, through His mighty power at work within us, to accomplish infinitely more than we might ask or think." Ephesians 3:20 (NLT)

It is so easy to doubt ourselves, but we need to understand the intentions that our Heavenly Father has for us. Whether great or small by the world's standards, our purposes are huge in God's kingdom. We see only a tiny portion of how He is using us and the impact we are having on those around us. But the ripples that spread out from our words and actions can have an impact far beyond our imaginations.

"Anything is possible if a person believes." Mark 9:23 (NLT) These words were spoken by Jesus in relation to His power to heal, but I trust they hold true in any situation. Every single time we speak an encouraging word, earnestly pray for a friend, or smile at a stranger, we are ministering the love of Christ. We are touching a life. And we have no idea how that person may be impacted to then inspire or encourage someone else.

Our lives matter! Our actions count! We can make a difference no matter who we are or what our situations may be. "Look around at the nations; look and be amazed! For I am doing something in your own day, something you wouldn't believe even if someone told you about it." Habakkuk 1:5 (NLT)

Perhaps you feel that your talents are nothing special. You may view yourself as ordinary in the eyes of others. However, never underestimate the extraordinary opportunities you have to shine brightly and produce a harvest in your unique sphere of influence.

Sometimes the gifts that come most naturally to us do not feel like gifts at all. For example, some might accomplish serving a meal or hosting a gathering at one's home with joy and ease. For others, it would be a stressful, nerve-wracking event. Hospitality does not come easily to all, but it is by no means trivial. Providing a warm, welcoming space for friends or family could have a lasting impact far beyond what we might ever know in this life.

We need to believe that using our gifts and talents and following Christ in the ways that He is leading us has significance. It matters to God and it matters to others—not just in this life. Incredibly, it is also of importance to those who have already passed before us.

The "Hall of Faith" chapter in Hebrews, which recalls the unbelievable displays of courage and belief by some of the most notable people mentioned in scripture, also says this: "All of these people we have mentioned received God's approval because of their faith, yet none of them received all that God had promised. For God had far better things in mind for us that would also benefit them, for they can't receive the prize at the end of the race until we finish the race." Hebrews 11:39-40 (NIV)

As Christians, it is as though we are all connected by an eternal God-chain. Imagine the colored construction paper chains that you may have made in your childhood. Now picture each loop as a person in God's kingdom. We are all connected together, carrying out

Christ's mission, each of us dependent on the one before us and the one after.

We can also visualize it as a relay race with each one of our lives representing one lap around the track; then we hand the baton off to the next person. Each one of us needs to finish our individual laps before the entire race is over and before the whole team can receive the prize.

In the kingdom of God, it is vital that we all put forth our best efforts to finish well, because our individual "races" affect the rest of the team. Although we may often feel as though our personal decisions affect only our own lives, it is beneficial to recognize that our influences, both positive and negative, stretch much further.

However, we need not fear that one slip-up will ruin eternity for everyone. In His gracious sovereignty, God has all of us covered with His forgiveness and love. Therefore, we need not be frightened or guilt-ridden. Rather, we can rejoice in knowing that we are all running the race together, picking each other up when one falls—cheering each other on if one becomes weary.

"So take a new grip with your tired hands and stand firm on your shaky legs. Mark out a straight path for your feet. Then those who follow you, though they are weak and lame, will not stumble and fall but will become strong." Hebrews 12:12-13 (NLT)

Let us always remember that each life has value and purpose, and is lovely and precious in God's sight. Psalm 139 tells us that the Lord's thoughts toward us are so numerous they cannot even be counted; they outnumber the grains of sand!

As we are trusting and believing God through each season of our lives, may we know in ever-greater measure that our Lord walks behind us, with us and ahead of us. Psalm 121 says, "The Lord shall preserve you from all evil; He shall preserve your soul. The Lord shall preserve your going out and your coming in from this time forth, and even forevermore." Psalm 121:7-8 (NKJV)

A friend shared these verses with me one time and said that she believes that the Lord is constantly serving us and that to preserve, or pre-serve, is like His going ahead of us to get everything ready before we get there. Knowing I was having a stressful week, she said, "I'll keep praying anyway, but He already has this week prepared for you."

God is continually pre-serving us. He is in complete control and He has every detail planned out. We just need to keep believing as He patiently and gently builds our faith.

During one of the many times that it seemed as though I had fallen down a hole in my trust-building journey, I felt God gently tugging at my heart, even in the midst of my angst. In my mind, I saw a picture of someone directing a car where the driver had just a few inches to go while parking. The person directing the driver was motioning with his hand, "Come on, come on, a little bit closer, just a little bit more."

That's what I felt God was saying to me. "Come on, keep coming, a little more, just a bit further. Keep trusting, keep believing. You're almost there."

Praising the Lord for what He has already completed in our lives is most certainly appropriate. However, it often takes little effort to be grateful *after* the blessing has been received, *after* the prayer has been answered, or *after* we have seen a positive outcome.

How much more compelling to worship in our darkest hour? How much greater if we risk believing beforehand? It is a powerful practice to trust God for an outcome before it happens. Can we praise Him during our deepest sorrow? Will we dare to believe when little hope is within sight?

As you move through this month of October, I encourage you to trust God in ever-deeper measures. See the incredibly vast plans that He has in store for you and for others. Believe that you are loved and valued, precious and worthy in His sight. Then prepare your grateful heart—for it's time to thank.

November: A time to thank

*"Then I will **thank** you in front of the great assembly. I will praise you before all the people."* Psalm 35:18 (NLT)

When we consider November, Thanksgiving is usually one of the first thoughts that springs to mind. Yet do we actually stop our busy lives in order to give heartfelt thanks? Or is Thanksgiving more a reminder that Christmas is fast approaching and we are already behind on our holiday preparations?

We readily complain about stores displaying Christmas items earlier and earlier and rushing the season. Though we are under no obligation to surrender to their marketing ploys, how often do we let this contribute to our stress levels and distract us from truly celebrating Thanksgiving?

In reality, every day should be a day to give thanks. Pausing for one Thursday in November surely does not reflect the honor and praise due our God for His daily care and provision in our lives.

I pray that I will never cease worshiping and thanking God for all He has accomplished in my life. May I praise Him privately and exalt Him publically. May my thanks be quiet and tender; may it be lavish and loud. May I bow low in reverence and raise my hands up high in jubilation. At all times, in all ways and in every circumstance—may I proclaim thanks.

God is deserving of our worship in every situation and season of our lives. Yet our thanksgiving tends to come more easily when life feels positive. Let us again learn from Job that God is to be praised in the arduous times as well.

After this man of God had lost nearly everything in one day, the Bible says he tore his robe and shaved his head. "Then he fell to the ground in worship." Job 1:20 (NIV) Not, he fell to the ground in despair—or in worry—or in anger. He fell to the ground in worship! After which Job spoke, "Naked I came from my mother's womb, and naked I will depart. The Lord gave and the Lord has taken away; may the name of the Lord be praised." Job 1:21 (NIV)

Job understood from the depths of his spirit that all he had and all that he was, came from God. He grasped fully that his family, his possessions and even his own life, were God's to do with as He pleased. In so doing, Job was free to give thanks even during the direst of conditions.

Although my first step might be to run toward God when troubles arise, I cannot say that I always come in worship. I pray that I can put these words into practice on a regular basis: "Rejoice always, pray continually, give thanks in all circumstances; for this is God's will for you in Christ Jesus." 1 Thessalonians 5:16-18 (NIV)

However, being thankful in all situations does not negate our other emotions. Jesus Himself experienced the full range of feelings from elation to anger, joy to sorrow. Emotions are most certainly from God and useful in numerous ways. Nevertheless, basing our decisions purely on how we feel or being in constant emotional turmoil is not a healthy way to live.

The instruction to rejoice always does not neglect the hurt, sadness, pain or guilt we may experience. Some situations will leave us devastated beyond words. However, in the core of our beings, in the center of our souls, where peace and hope reside—is also the birthplace of thanks. Knowing and trusting that our heavenly Daddy loves us greatly and cares for us deeply, allows us to give thanks when every outward circumstance would indicate a different response.

Job was praising from that deep place of trust. That same level of gratitude is also attainable for us. Choosing thanks in the midst of sorrow is one of the purest forms of praise we can offer. And by the Holy Spirit's power and support, it is available to us at any and all times.

Giving thanks immediately should be our foremost priority regardless of the situation. Knowing that God sees our needs, hears our prayers and understands our hearts can help us to be grateful at all times.

"Don't worry about anything; instead, pray about everything. Tell God what you need, and thank him for all he has done. Then you will experience God's peace, which exceeds anything we can understand. His peace will guard your hearts and minds as you live in Christ Jesus." Philippians 4:6-7 (NLT)

Along with giving thanks in the present, we should also be grateful when looking back at past circumstances. Often these are the moments when we can catch a glimpse into "all things working together for good."

Never in my wildest imagination would I have dreamed that one day I would be giving thanks for the "smoking people." I will readily confess that I was not rejoicing, praising or thanking during their time of living next door. However, I am very pleased to report that afterwards, I was able to see the blessing that had been provided.

In order to assist with clearing out the smoke, we purchased two air cleaners. Much to our delight, we discovered that not only did they help with the smoke—they assisted greatly in managing our dear kitty Braveheart's asthma condition. Never on our own would we have considered such a purchase. Without them, we truly believe Bravey's health would be far greater compromised. So thank you, "smoking people." And thank you Lord!

I pray that this experience will remind me to be grateful and thankful in all situations and circumstances, knowing that the One who holds the future also cradles me in the present.

It is also vital that we remember what God has done for us in the past, in order to build our hope for the future. This process was put into practice by the Israelites in Joshua, Chapter 4. After they had crossed the Jordan River with the Ark of the Covenant, they built a memorial with twelve stones that they took from the middle of the dry riverbed.

Joshua told the people, "In the future, your children will ask, 'What do these stones mean?' Then you can tell them, 'This is where the Israelites crossed the Jordan on dry ground. For the Lord your God dried up the river right before your eyes, and he kept it dry until you were all across, just as he did at the Red Sea when he dried it up until we had all crossed over. He did this so that all the nations of the earth might know the power of the Lord, and that you might fear the Lord your God forever.'" Joshua 4:21-24 (NLT)

When the Lord does something amazing in your life, build a memorial so you will never forget. Then during the trying times, you can pull out your stones and remember. You can know with a certainty in your soul that even though you may be standing before a rushing river, when you take that first step of faith and get your toes wet, you will walk across on dry ground. For God will lead you to the other side.

Remembering what God has accomplished for us in the past can bring great comfort when dealing with trials that might take place years later. Our memories quickly fade and we so easily forget when new difficulties overtake us. Those are the times to hold our memorial stones close to our hearts, to read and reread our journals, and to refresh our remembrances. In so doing, we can reflect on the past, gain hope for the future, and be thankful in the present.

Those memories can also help us to encourage and bless others. Without the trying situations in my life over the past fifteen years, I would have little hope or comfort to offer to others. I am truly grateful for all God has brought Doug and me through these many years. My faith has been enlarged and my life is fuller and richer than the more shallow existence I had been living. I can more closely relate to others battling difficulties and pray for them in confidence and faith, because of God's faithfulness in my own journey.

So often, we wish for an easy life, devoid of trouble. Yet where would the growth be? And would we truly be content? Adam and Eve prove that we would not. As the first-born of all creation, they had a perfect life. Everything in their surroundings was pure and flawless. Yet they were not satisfied. Why do we believe we would feel otherwise?

Only through tremendous friction and irritation does the oyster create the pearl. We too can shimmer and shine as precious gems when we allow God to transform us from dust to glory. "To all who mourn in Israel, He will give a crown of beauty for ashes, a joyous blessing instead of mourning, festive praise instead of despair. In their righteousness, they will be like great oaks that the Lord has planted for His own glory." Isaiah 61:3 (NLT)

How can we not be thankful? All of creation was formed to offer praise back to God. Jesus told the Pharisees if His followers remained quiet, the stones themselves would cry out. Isaiah tells us, "The mountains and hills will burst into song, and the trees of the field will clap their hands!" Isaiah 55:12 (NLT)

If nature itself cannot help but praise the God who created it, why should we be any different? If our own words are lacking, the Psalms are rich in songs of praise. Psalm 148 shows the breadth by which all of heaven and earth are to praise our glorious God. From the sun and moon and twinkling stars, to the creatures of the ocean depths. From small, scurrying animals and birds, to the kings of the earth and all people. Wind and weather, snow and clouds, mountains and hills. ALL are to praise the Lord! Indeed, He is worthy of our praise.

This November, as you plan your Thanksgiving meal with family and friends, take some time to give thanks. Then keep on rejoicing.

For every day, there is reason to worship. Each moment is an opportunity to exalt. Every season brings an occasion to praise. And as the year draws to a close, it is time to reflect.

Epilogue: A time to reflect

"I will study your commandments and reflect on your ways. I will delight in your decrees and not forget your word." Psalm 119:15-16 (NLT)

"There is a time for everything, a season for every activity under heaven." Ecclesiastes 3:1 (NLT) Indeed, our lives ebb and flow and our emotions rise and fall as we journey through peaks and valleys. Yet one constant remains. Through every season of our souls, our loving God journeys with us.

He laughs with us in delight and cries with us in despair. He hopes with us when we wonder and waits for us when we wander. He loves us though we feel unlovable and esteems us though we feel unworthy.

In every time and in every season—God is faithful.

As I closed my eyes and listened to Chris Tomlin's song "Faithful," snapshots of my life sprang to mind, frame by frame. I glimpsed moments of great joy and memories of tremendous sorrow. Like a line graph, I both viewed and felt the ups and downs of the many emotions of my life's travels and travails.

Then, in a beautiful overlay, I saw God's faithfulness covering every single image. In every moment, in every instance—He was there. He was there, He was there, He was there. During that time of reflection, I recognized more fully than ever, that God was truly with me at all times, in all ways, and in all seasons.

He is always loving, ever caring and forever faithful. As we move through the various physical and spiritual times of our lives, we are never alone. And when we delight in the Lord both day and night, this shall be said of us: "They are like trees planted along the riverbank, bearing fruit each season. Their leaves never wither, and they prosper in all they do." Psalm 1:3 (NLT)

May we bloom all year round, as we love, trust and follow our beautiful Savior. Thank you for journeying with me.

In all times and in every season—may you be blessed.

CPSIA information can be obtained
at www.ICGtesting.com
Printed in the USA
BVHW072202181118
532975BV00001B/15/P